THE *O*prahfication OF OUR Culture

BY CHERYL INGRAM

The Oprahfication of Our Culture

ISBN 0-88144-305-0
Copyright © 2008 by Cheryl Ingram

Published by
IMI Publishing
P. O. Box 10261
Daytona Beach, FL 32120

Packaged & Printed By
Victory Graphics and Media
9731 East 54th Street
Tulsa, OK 74146
www.victorygraphicsandmedia.com

Table of Contents

Acknowledgements

One Sunday afternoon I had the house to myself and I was piddling in the kitchen with the big screen television blaring in the background. I was half listening to T.D. Jakes preaching a message about making the main thing the main thing, about getting back to your first love. In my mind and heart I was telling the Lord how weary I was with all the business and pressure of the ministry. I was whining about songs I am writing that are not finished and need to be recorded and about books inside my spirit that I want to get written. I felt a compelling to get these things completed, but constrained by ministry obligations.

Suddenly, T. D. Jakes looked into the camera and said something to the effect, *Listen to me preacher. You are so busy doing things for God that you haven't spent time with him the way you used to. You are so tired and weary of the business of the ministry you can't worship the way you used to. Do you hear me? You finish writing those songs. You get that book written if it never gets published!*

The hair on the back of my neck and my arms stood straight up. I literally looked around the room expecting to see the Lord, or at least an angel. I threw up my hands and worshipped God and committed to get it done. So I want to thank T. D. Jakes for obeying God and speaking out what he heard. I know his words ministered to thousands, but his stern proclamation was a specific assignment for me. I began working on this book right away.

I also want to thank my handsome, intelligent and talented son, Steve Jr., for respecting my teaching. I believe he has a great future beyond anything that he can ask or even think. Finally, I thank my long time partner and husband, Dr. Steve Ingram, for believing in my calling and encouraging me to accomplish it. Thank-you for our morning and afternoon power walks where our discussions helped to articulate my thoughts into words. I love you.

CHAPTER ONE

Oprahfication

A television show that, arguably, has defined an entire generation is *Saturday Night Live.* The humorist skits portrayed could be described as quirky, profane, and awkwardly satirical. It is a program of definite memorable moments and characters. Perhaps you, like millions of other people, have recited a one liner from a *Saturday Night Live* skit and caused your immediate audience to break out in laughter. The creators, writers and actors of this program have successfully lampooned current events, political figures, and personalities and the creative sketches reveal insight to our culture. In one particular act, the characters portrayed Oprah Winfrey, the famous talk show host and owner of a media empire, as the Queen hoisted on an Egyptian carriage by four slaves who balanced her and the structure on their shoulders. Chants of O-PRAH, O-PRAH, O-PRAH filled the sound as everyone bowed to her. It was funny.

Why is it comical? We laugh because the goddess like frenzy, the idol worship over Oprah does strike some as extreme. Oprah fans would decry the skit irreverent. She is

Oprah Winfrey, a Black woman who rose from the ashes of poverty, sexual abuse and prejudice to achieve what so few accomplish, male or female, Black or Caucasian. Through education and determination she took advantage of opportunities and has become a very wealthy media mogul. Women admire her because she is like US. She struggles with her weight. She has a best girlfriend. She wears false eyelashes and sometimes lets us see her without make-up. She loves animals, particularly her dogs. She gives great advice. She has the best guests. She gave away how many cars? Everybody loves Oprah. Don't you love Oprah?

Don't you love Oprah?

Of course! What red blooded American woman doesn't love Oprah? Who doesn't look forward to that afternoon in front of your television set to see what her topic will be today and who she will be interviewing? She is so comfortable in her own skin. She is so comfortable in front of the camera. We feel like we're in her living room and she has invited us to spend some time with her and she really is our friend. She really cares about us.

It is sincere. It is not about the money or the fame. It is about her fulfilled purpose on this earth. She believes to whom much is given much is required. She knows she has prominence and fortune so that she can give back to humanity. This is her destiny. I respect her greatly for that. Her charitable donations and philanthropic efforts are to be commended. She has brought awareness and solutions to problems faced by so many individuals, not only by discussing them on her program, but by providing solutions. She has sent in the Calvary, so to speak, to ravaged areas such as New Orleans after Hurricane Katrina, and is making a difference in millions of lives through the Angel Network. Her Leadership Academy for Girls in South Africa is assisting young women there to become leaders worldwide. Oprah Winfrey has tremendous influence and the wealth to make things happen. She has made screen stars out of unknown personalities. Whatever book she recommends for her book club can catapult an author and his/her writings out of obscurity onto the Best Sellers list. She even has enough influence to help convince a United States Senator, a Black man, to run for the office of the President.

Oddly, it is her influence that presents the greatest caution I can express. Oprah is not God. She is not perfect. She is not always right. Her opinions are just that...her opinions. When her views do not line up with the Word of God, we as believing Believers should address it. She is influencing an entire generation with an ideology that is often contrary to our firmly held beliefs. Oprah Winfrey was reared in traditional Christianity, but over the years has allegedly embraced New Age philosophies, the Secret, and many other mystical, metaphysical, non-Christian ideals. These views are underscored on her programs and in her magazine. She has not, to the best of my knowledge, married her long time live in partner, Stedman Graham. To be fair, they may have a contractual arrangement that we know nothing about,

Oprah is
not God

but their relationship has not been a traditional marriage by any stretch of imagination. I viewed one program where she surprised a couple whose apartment was across the way from her Chicago Harpo Studios. They could actually view her buildings from their home, and they stated they were living together there, not married. Oprah looked into the camera and said something to the effect, *Well, you know I'm OK with that. I'm all for that.*

Some, but certainly not all, of Oprah Winfrey's opinions represent a part of the current cultural climate which paints Christians and our traditional stands as being archaic, homophobic, out of touch, prejudiced, and uncompromising. Some determine us archaic because we revere the Bible as the final authority. Many dismiss it as being a compilation of poetry, history and prose, but certainly not the Word of God. They deem it a good book, but not the sole source of their spirituality. They point to many writings of other religions and revelations. If they believe in God at all, they relay that God is certainly a big God and He must have revealed Himself to others who have interpreted Him differently.

We are described as being homophobic because we regard definite passages of scripture outlining sexual activity between men and men and women and women as a sinful, abhorrent lifestyle. We are said to be out of touch because we are not expanding our thinking on morality with the rest of the world as it evolves. We are said to be narrow minded because in the culture's view we do not accept other religions as valid. The culture dictates that we embrace all ideas, all religions no matter if they are directly opposed to our beliefs, that we must keep an open mind. Compromise is the catch phrase. The current culture wants traditional Christians to let go of our convictions in order to broaden our friendships and deepen our relationships.

These cultural ideas are espoused by television personalities and many in the educational and Hollywood communities. Actors and famous stars are attractive. We want to look like them, be cool like them, and have money like them. We love to hear their success stories, don't we? However I have questions about these artisans. Most of them cannot stay married. Most have relationships and even children without marriage. These relationships do not hold up under the pressure and schedule of their lives. Why then do we admire and revere them as examples of possessing ideal, loving relationships, albeit however brief? Many of these stars freely express their opinions on politics, religion and other spiritual and moral matters. How does memorizing some lines and pretending to be someone you are not qualify you to be somehow more enlightened and informed? How does working in an industry of make believe cause that person to become an expert on very serious spiritual matters?

The cultural community does not understand how those of us with traditional Biblical values hold these convictions very deeply in the core of our inner man, and why we are sincerely repulsed by their ever widening boundaries of decency. There seems to be no more limits to public profanity, morality, and humiliating, verbal assaults on Christians. My concern is that if we do not respond to the constant barrage of criticism, we are holding up a white flag to the enemy of our faith. Please understand we do not war against people. Oprah Winfrey is not the enemy, but when she and others oppose standards of the Word of God and give validity to their own philosophies simply by their popularity, Christian leaders have a right and the authority to expose the error. The public's enamor with popular personalities is indicative of times in which we live. Our culture is in desperate need of sanctification, a cleansing, a washing through God's Word. Instead we are experiencing an oprafication—if not an outright acceptance of values that are foreign to Christians worldwide then certainly an indifference to them. Corinthians 10:3, 4 in the Message Bible states,

> *The world is unprincipled. It's dog-eat-dog out there! The world doesn't fight fair. But we don't live or fight our battles that way—never have and never will. The tools of our trade aren't for marketing or manipulation, but they are for demolishing that entire massively corrupt culture.*

The emphasis is on massively corrupt culture. Some would point to historical periods of history where cultures were perhaps just as debase and pronounced. Yes, and they no longer exist. Their culture was also their demise. Certain forms and practices of pagan worship and idolatry may be in some ways extinct, however their spiritual roots remain. We will deal with some of those roots. The concepts of cultural idealism we currently face are not new. As you read on, I will trace their origins and I will be very candid and transparent as I relay my own experiences. You may think it intriguing that I

call this *The Oprahfication of Our Culture,* but
I do so because I am genuinely concerned
that we must express the truth. In an era
when we as Christians should be concen-
trating on purification and dedication we
seem to be mesmerized by opinions of
pundits. We know inherently that some of
these ideas do not agree with what God's

Word says, yet we often fall in line with the cultural fan club. I
believe it is imperative now more than ever that we heed the
words preached by our ministers and Christian leaders over
those spoken by cultural idols. We must let our own voices be
heard over the noise of the cultural elite even if it sounds like
only a whisper.

CHAPTER TWO

Come Meet a Man

OK. If you got past the first chapter you might already have decided that I am a typical idealistic "born again" churchgoer with an anti-cultural agenda. Let me assure you this book is not intended to be condescending or judgmental. You may ask, *Why would you take on such a controversial topic?* The answer is quite simple, *How can they hear without a preacher?*[1] Unless people are told the truth by preachers who are willing to speak the truth, they will continue in a downward spiral of moral decay.

I am a preacher who understands that people are valuable, born with insecurities, flaws or "issues" if you will. I can certainly identify with those frailties. I have not led a sheltered life. Though I have a godly mother and though my maternal grandfather was a pastor, I was raised in a home with an alcoholic abusive father. I know what it is to be in fear of someone you are supposed to love, to be embarrassed by that person's behavior, and to watch them squander financial and other material resources in order to satisfy the craving for that next drink. While my father was a financially generous man, I have vivid memories of vulgar conversations and irrational behavior induced by a chemical substance. I have not been shielded from the unseemly or obscene.

I made it through the maze and found my way to Christ, or I should say He found me. My husband and I dedicated our lives to God as young people and have traveled this world obeying that call. I am a Co-Pastor. Real pastors must receive people with open arms and have the ability to reach across a broad spectrum of society embracing all kinds of personalities. Pastors are shepherds who lovingly care for sheep—straying sheep, lost sheep, hurt sheep. Pastors smell like sheep. They live with the sheep, eat with the sheep, play with the sheep and minister to the sheep. My husband and I have been overtly generous with church members and most people we meet. Our hearts long to help people. We firmly believe that one does not need to have participated in a wrong behavior in order to identify with a person's pain. In other words, we don't need to have committed the sin in order to know how it feels. We see the hurt. We want to help fix it. We see wrong behavior and we want to help correct it, because we recognize it will only bring more pain.

Someone once told me that a pastor does not make a good administrator, because pastors see a person's potential and not who they currently are, or who a person can become, not who they are right now. Pastors who make personnel decisions based on a person's potential will most likely see that employee fail. Administrators, on the other hand, make measured decisions on how productive or useful a person will be in the immediate. I have found that to be so. My husband has the true heart of a pastor. He sees the best in every person. He will come to your defense no matter what you may have done.

The Great Pastor, The Good Shepherd, Jesus Christ, believed the best of people and even He made some seemingly unwise personnel decisions. He had a treasurer who was robbing from the purse and ultimately sold him out for thirty pieces of silver. One disciple who was first to recognize him as the Messiah, eventually denied him, cursed people out and cut off a soldier's ear. Literally all of his twelve disciples abandoned him in his greatest hour of need. What a mess these guys were, yet he loved them and died for them. The Bible describes Christ as the one who took a whip, threw out the greedy money changers from the temple and conversely sat children in his lap and embraced them. He is shown as a lover of people who loves enough to point out their weaknesses so that he can minister His love to them.

He Changed Women

In one account, the men of the city dragged a prostitute in front of Him demanding that she be punished, stoned to death. He picked up a stone and said, *Let him who is without sin throw the first stone.* Each man in turn walked away acknowledging they were just as guilty. After all, how did they know she was a prostitute anyway? They most likely had benefited from her services. Jesus didn't condone her sin or their sin, but He loved her enough to say, *Go and sin no more.*[2] In other words, *There is a better way to live than this. You are better than this.* What compassion to reveal the shortcoming and point to a way out.

Another woman had her life completely changed by Christ's mercy. While in the public square at the watering well (not secluded in the temple), Jesus met a woman and had an interesting conversation with her. How radical it was for Him to break through the gender barrier and then the racial barrier. It was against religious tradition for a man to speak to a woman and against racial tradition for a Jew to

There is a better way

speak to a lower class Samaritan. She was quite shocked. He simply asked for a drink of water then revealed who He really was—the long awaited Messiah. He proved it by telling her to go get her husband. She told him she didn't have a husband and then he "read her mail." He said, *That's right you don't have a husband. But, you've had five husbands and the man you currently live with is not your husband.* Jesus didn't say this to condemn but to help her escape the destructive way she was living. She believed on Him.

He said something to her that I believe was the convincing point. He told her that the Samaritans, her people, worshipped God on one mountain while the Jews worshipped God at another but, *There is coming a day when all will worship the Father in spirit and in truth.* Jesus revealed Himself as the Son of God, the Truth. Just like the woman at the well the world around us needs a fresh revelation that

Jesus Christ is God. Without that knowledge they will continue to live their lives void of conscience.

Christ helped her understand that she must worship God out of her own spirit, not just in the form of a religious ceremony or dogma, and she must worship Him in TRUTH. The truth must be spoken so that redemption and true worship can occur. He had to bring attention to the TRUTH of her lifestyle so that He could show her the answer of what true worship is. Pastors teach and preach the TRUTH out of love for hurting people.

She ran to her friends and family and said, *Come meet a man who told me everything I have ever done!* The townspeople came and Jesus ministered to them as well, spending two full days changing their lives.[3]

*Come meet a man...*I have met that man. Jesus said in another place, *I am the Way and the Truth and the Life; no one comes to the Father except by (through) Me.* John 14:6 AMP

Just as Jesus revealed the sin in order to save the lost, I am convinced that we must raise consciousness to our own subtle apathy. It takes pastors, preachers, to tell people the truth so that real change can occur. The old story says that if you put a frog in a pot of boiling hot water he'll jump out immediately. If you put a frog in a pot of cold water and gradually turn up the temperature he'll stay in that pot and die, because his body adjusts to the heat. Like the frog, we are gradually being desensitized—oprahtized—to the culture around us.

Oprah-tized to the culture

Some believe that mankind is inherently good, that we are ever evolving, expanding, growing into better human beings. In reality the opposite is true. We are all flawed human beings born into a sinful society who need a Savior. I needed a Savior and I met Him in Jesus Christ. I don't much care for religion. Neither did He. He broke through man-made religious boundaries in order to deliver people from bondage. It is through the love and ministry of Christ that I hope to shine light on the dark side of our culture, helping some in the process to find hope instead of despair, a hand to hold and a guide to show the way out of that downward cycle. Yes, our culture has devolved and, in other ways, we are experiencing the same demonic influences of generations past.

I want to delve into some of that historical information, but first let's give definition to the problem.

CHAPTER THREE
The Devolving Culture

Many theologians and ministers are espousing that we are now living in a post modern or post Christian society. They point to the culture in European countries and in the United States of America that no longer recognizes the importance of the organized religion that has become Christianity. The cultural elite in Europe and Hollywood have been portrayed as applauding the leaning away from traditional Christianity citing it as an improvement, a move into a more positive direction. I define this new cultural code as the Devolving Culture.

As wonderful a person as Oprah Winfrey is, many of the ideas preached from her pulpit, which she allegedly believes have merit and deserve a voice and credence, represent thinking of the Devolving Culture. These ideas are in direct opposition to traditional Biblical Christian standards. She has given many of these ideas a public forum on her television show. We have viewed stories of individuals who unashamedly speak of their fornicating behavior which drew wide acceptance from the studio audience. We have seen homosexual partners telling their stories, which evoked great sympathy and admiration from Oprah's audience. We have watched husbands and wives revealing that after years of marriage they discover they are "gay" and must divorce so that they can be true to themselves. One show highlighted a middle aged woman author who has written about her many sexual relationships with multiple partners. She had a captive audience in which she preached her own behavior as a liberating experience recommended for all women who desired freedom from backward social mores. She declared, after all, middle aged women can enjoy sex without commitment as much as middle aged men.

While I am quite confident that Oprah would never endorse pornography, violence or any illegal activity, proponents of the Devolving Culture would adhere to a doctrine of each individual being in control of his or her own moral compass, that all opinions are equal. As long as one is a law abiding citizen, a good person, helping his/her fellow man, contributing to society and as long as one's personal behavior does not infringe on the rights of another, you have no authority to judge or condemn them. All religions are of benefit as long as they are helping the individuals who receive from those religious teachings. As long as one believes in some kind of "higher power" he is on his own path to righteousness. How one defines that "higher power" is of little consequence. It is not the definition, but the believing that matters, and as long as one believes, you have no right to impose your personal religious beliefs, especially if those views are Biblically oriented. The cultural elite or those who adhere to the Devolving Culture would depict an open mind and acceptance of most ideas, except when those ideas infringe on their own desired behavior. When this mindset is confronted with opinions backed by scripture the mindset labels those opinions as being intolerant.

So according to this mindset, if you choose to use profanity in a public place or on television go ahead. What's a little curse word here and there going to hurt anybody? It's your prerogative to speak as you please, and if someone around you doesn't like it they can get off their indignant high horse and kiss your #&*! They reason that people are going to curse. It's a fact of life. But this same philosophy often will not tolerate a Christian praying or quoting the Bible out loud in the same public place. They also reason that as long as you believe that a fetus is not a human being you can "remove it" without conviction and refuse to hear a lecture on the sanctity of the unborn. Further, they expect public tax dollars to fund abortions of those less fortunate, no matter who disagrees with their opinion. They reason that people are going to have sex, so sexual activity should be accepted without judgment and if pregnancy occurs there should be safe and inexpensive remedies.

The more widespread this doctrine the further our society declines into moral decay and the more desensitized and accepting we become.

I'm OK

There was a book written years ago entitled, *I'm OK, You're OK*.[4] That phrase sums up the Devolving Culture. Everyone is

OK as long as they are a good person and not hurting anyone else. As long as your behavior isn't hurting anyone your behavior is OK. The problem with this mindset is that everyone is not OK. There are consequences to violating scriptural principles. There is a standard of absolutes. There is a real God. Jesus Christ is the Son of God. Jesus and His Word are one and the same. When you violate His Word you violate Him. When you turn a deaf ear to His Word you grieve His Holy Spirit.

Josh McDowell, who has represented Campus Crusade for Christ, speaking to more than ten million young people in eighty-four countries, including more than 700 university and college campuses is well respected. "As a skeptic at Kellogg College in Michigan, he was challenged by a group of Christian students to examine intellectually the claims of Christianity. He accepted the challenge and set out to prove that Christ's claims to be God and the historical reliability of Scripture could be neither trusted nor accurately verified. The evidence he discovered changed the course of his life. He discovered that the Bible was the most historically reliable document of all antiquity and that Christ's claim that He was God was true. That brought him to the inescapable conclusion that Christ loved him and died to redeem him."[5]

In his book *The Last Christian Generation*,[6] Josh McDowell outlines the current cultural phenomenon as being a distinct redefinition of terms. He says this emerging generation hears the same words, but interprets them differently. Our society has changed the definitions. Here is an example of the differences:

Word	Traditional Values	Devolving Culture
Tolerance	I accept you but I don't share your beliefs. I don't agree with your lifestyle.	I accept your beliefs and choices, because all beliefs are equal.
Respect	I respect your beliefs but I don't approve.	I completely approve of your choices, beliefs or lifestyle.
Morality	I believe in morality as determined by God.	I have no right to judge another person's view or behavior.
Sexual Morality	I only have sex with my husband/wife.	I only have sex with someone I love.
Personal Rights	I have a right to be treated fairly under the law.	I have a right do whatever I think is best for me and if necessary change the law.
Truth	I believe in absolute standards of right and wrong.	I believe that truth is relative. You define your own truth.

I cannot improve on how Josh McDowell has articulated this explanation so I will just quote him. Speaking of the youth culture which I have labeled as the Devolving Culture, "It would be hard to argue against their viewpoint if Christianity was merely a system of beliefs as they have been led to believe. If Christianity was based solely on ethical teachings or theological concepts, then they'd be right—it would be one competing religion among many from which to choose...But Christianity isn't a mere religion, and it is not simply based upon various teachings. Christianity is based on the life, character, and identity of a person—Jesus Christ. Christ did not come to earth to teach Christianity—Christ is Christianity. That is what makes Christianity unique. It is a personal relationship with the personal creator God. Most religions of the world are based on philosophical propositions or theological ideologies. Remove its founding prophet or guru and that religion remains essentially intact. That is because these religions are based on the teachings, not upon the founding teacher.

That is not true of Christianity. While the Christian faith has a particular belief system and people have developed a theological construct from Scripture, its essential basis is the life, work, and person of its founder—Jesus Christ. This unique fact fundamentally changes the discussion. Instead of comparing the teachings of one religion to another, the essential question in Christianity is how a man or woman relates to the person of Jesus Christ. Remove Christ from Christianity, and you lose the entire meaning of biblical faith. As the apostle Paul said, if Christ isn't who he claimed to be and if he did not rise from the dead, then *our message has no meaning and your faith also has no meaning* (1 Corinthians 15:14 GWT/God's Word Translation)."[7]

It's All About Jesus Christ

For those of us who are traditional Biblical Christianity proponents, it's all about Jesus Christ. Everything we believe, every behavior, every decision boils down to our personal relationship with the Son of God. Unless the Devolving Culture experiences that radical transformation from sin consciousness to righteousness consciousness we are simply in a war of words with them. It is a matter of a heart transplant, the heart of Father God being transplanted into our very spirit being. Born again—that phrase alone conjures arguments. However, when one is truly born again of the Holy Spirit you will have a radical purging of wrong thoughts, ideas, and behaviors. We receive the mind of Christ and are transformed from darkness into light, from death to life, and from defeat to victory.

This war of words must be fought. We who believe the Word of God are discussing issues with those of the Devolving Culture who hear the same words but interpret them differently. That's why our children can reject what we have taught them without conviction. They are not hearing what has been said, but instead are acting on what they hear filtered through the current corrupt culture. We must continue to define the truth. We must outline the consequences of disobedience to the truth.

A war of words

The Prophet Isaiah foretold of the end times when gross darkness would cover the earth, and Jesus described the climate, social and political conditions occurring before He would physically return for His Church.[8] I believe we are the generation Isaiah and Christ predicted would see His return. The world has certainly known perversion and filthy behavior in times past, but never in our history has the entire globe been so bankrupt of moral fiber. The wonderful aspect of God's Word is that when He gives us insight into the future it is never without hope.

Arise, shine; for thy light is come, and the glory of the LORD
is risen upon thee. For, behold, the darkness shall cover the earth,
and gross darkness the people: but the LORD shall arise upon thee,
and his glory shall be seen upon thee.

(Isaiah 60:1 and 2 KJV)

As long as there is breath in born again Believers there is light in this darkness and we are light in the midst of the Devolving Culture. As Jesus told us we cannot hide our light under a bushel.[9] We must let it shine for all to see, even if we are being ridiculed and belittled. In fact, shine brighter. Speak up…a little louder…a little louder…

CHAPTER FOUR

Getting to the Roots

The Devolving Culture is akin to a cancerous mass spreading throughout our society. A cancerous growth multiplies and spreads until it invades and destroys other vital organs. If it can be detected and removed in its early stages the prognosis is usually favorable. Left to linger without serious medical intervention the human body will succumb to its deadly outcome. Cancer must be dealt with from the root. Modern medical techniques wipe out cancer cells through chemotherapy and radiation treatments which destroy not only the cancerous cells, the root, but good cells as well. These treatments are toxic and sometimes do more damage to the patient than the cancer itself. This is a radical but often necessary solution. Unfortunately, the culture's demise is far too advanced for simple surgery.

Oh, come on, it's not that serious some would argue. Really? Well, as the cigarette commercial once decried, *We've come a long way baby!* Not too many years ago an Oscar winning movie, *Gone With the Wind,* evoked a huge controversy for using the one word "damn" in its dialogue. Fast forward to the movies produced in today's culture and the dialogue would make a crusty old sailor blush. There are no more limitations to the boundaries of verbal discretion on the various media outlets—internet, satellite radio, and web casting. Live television and radio programs take a risk every time they invite a guest to be interviewed. People are emboldened now to say whatever they want and the federally regulated agencies don't appear to be keeping up with broken standards of decency.

The average man or woman on the street mirrors what they see and hear in the media. You can be standing in line at the grocery store, the movies, the mall or a restaurant and hear all sorts of indecent language in front of you and your children. People are talking the way they are believing. This is what is IN them. Jesus Christ told us that a good man speaks good words and an evil man speaks evil words that *...out of the abundance (overflow) of the heart his mouth speaks.* (Luke 6:46 AMP) The Psalmist referred to an evil speaking man saying *...He clothed himself also with cursing as with his garment, and it seeped into his inward [life] like water, and like oil into his bones.* (Psalm 109:18 AMP) Did you get that? In other words, people are cursing from the inside out, not the outside in. Fowl, obscene language has gotten INSIDE! Profanity has cancerously invaded the bone marrow of the body of society. In order to get to the root of the problem, it requires a radical procedure.

Profanity has invaded

Profuse Profanity

Contestants in the Miss America pageant typically have a platform or a cause for which they commit to be an advocate, such as aids research, cancer research, domestic abuse awareness, etc. I have stated that I think a great cause would be awareness to eliminate public profanity. Can you imagine how a beautiful young lady would be ridiculed for even suggesting such a position? She would probably be laughed out of the competition.

Some years ago before we began pastoring our church, my husband and I traveled in full time music and teaching ministry. We had to catch one of those red eye flights, an early morning before the sun comes up flight, and everyone was quietly and sleepily boarding the plane. This was at a time before the airlines had stringent Homeland Security policies in place and I am confident what occurred would not take place today. The two of us were seated in the bulkhead at the very front of the coach cabin. Steve put his bags in the overhead compartment, got out his Bible and notepad and settled in to study and I was going to take a good nap when on board came a group of men who had obviously been up all night drinking, having participated in some sports event. They were loudly spewing the most disgusting, bar room, obscene talk, oblivious to others. People were uncomfortable, but no one spoke thinking they would take their seats and be more respectful of those around them. They got worse and louder. My husband said squirming in his seat. *I'm going to say something.* He squirmed some more. *I'm going to say something.* I looked at him and said, *No, let me.* All five foot 2½ plus inches of me stood up, turned around to where they were in the middle of the coach cabin and yelled out, *Well, Praise God,* and then I proceeded to speak in other tongues as the Holy Spirit gave me utterance to the top of my voice, finishing with *Hallelujah! Thank-you Jesus!* I sat down and the plane suddenly went silent. Ha! Go figure! A few moments later the flight attendant came over to us, leaned down and said, *Thank-you!* We had a very quiet ride to our destination.

Radical? You bet. I had a choice to sit there and allow the voice of our culture to dominate my environment or take drastic measures and throw some spiritual chemo and radiation treatment on the subjects. I dumped the whole load. It killed that cancer. The men took their seats, went to sleep and didn't say another word the whole trip. When we disembarked to collect our luggage those same men were sheepishly much more respectful. They had probably never had that happen to them before. I certainly had never done it before (but I have done it since). Now when someone uses profanity in front of me, I just speak praise to God right out loud. If they can speak vile words, I can speak life giving words.

Cancerous Lifestyles

It goes deeper than just some evil speaking though. This cancer is a mindset that spills over into all areas. Parents can no longer discipline children for fear of repercussions of child abuse. We have many educators in our congregation who convey their frustrations of inadequacy in controlling their classrooms for fear of reprisals. Consequently, the lack of respect that children have for authority is out of control. Most parents and teachers no longer use the Bible as a source to instruct children in ways of conduct. There is no current written standardized code of conduct that all of society adheres to, since The Ten Commandments, our long standing Judeo/Christian guideline has been removed from the public forum. People are left to decide for themselves what behavior is correct for them.

Children are having children. Our culture promotes the display of graphic scenes of lurid, sexual behavior on movie and television and computer screens, and try as we may to prevent it, our children have easy access to it. They simply act out what they see without maturity to process the magnitude of their actions. Without the

Children are having children

moral guidelines to steer them toward healthier decisions, they will act out of their carnal impulses every time. Contraceptives or abortion clinics are readily available without parental consent, so there is no person of authority to be accountable to. Society has rationalized that kids are going to have sex, so we have to accept it as fact and assist them in the repercussions. The culture acknowledges this sexual behavior and then paradoxically acts outraged when a sexual pervert rapes and kills women and children. It is a cancer of moral decline spinning in a vortex toward destruction.

Many parents have resigned themselves to accepting the new social code so as not to alienate their children who live together unmarried. There used to be a stigma associated with two people who choose to live together. Not too long ago, one was generally considered lower class, debase, and morally corrupt who engaged in such behavior. You didn't even have to be a churchgoer. Society dictated a standard that everyone adhered to. Today more and more people are deciding to cohabit, without marriage, bringing even more confusion to the family unit as they merge their families. According to a recent article by Rochelle Sharpe in *USA Weekend,*[10] "nearly 40% of U.S. babies were born out of wedlock in 2006, an all-time high, government statistics show." The same article states that young women between the ages of 25-29 represent the fastest growing group of unwed mothers. These women adhere to the new mindset of cohabitation in lieu of or in postponement of marriage, choosing to live with their boyfriends. Some say we are spawning a generation of bastards, but in reality there are no illegitimate children, only promiscuous parents.

Unfortunately, there is now an anti-Christ spirit permeating our culture that is more and more desensitized to wrong moral conduct. Christian bashing, mocking, ridiculing and blatant disregard for our values is all too common. Two recent movies help to make my point. The first movie was rated R, which means you must be 17 years of age to be admitted. (We all know that kids younger than that see these films via the internet or DVD eventually.) I refused to see it because I don't enjoy the moronic filthy humor the producer is known for and because I had heard about some controversial scenes of nudity. I asked the person who saw it if it indeed had scenes of full frontal nudity. When he replied that it did with both men and women, my immediate response was, *How do they get away with that? That is pornographic display in a regular theater!* Our culture thinks it's amusing. Our children have come to accept it as normal.

The second movie was recommended by Oprah Winfrey. She espoused it as being one of the best movies of the year and it was indeed nominated for several Academy Awards. Somehow I convinced my husband to go with me and he actually sat through the whole thing, not because he was enjoying it but because he knew I was doing research for this book. It is the story of a 16 year old girl who has sex with her geeky boyfriend one time, gets pregnant from that encounter and decides to put the baby up for adoption. I thought it might be a sweet film to enlighten young women about the real consequences of engaging in adult sexual behavior. On the contrary, I found it to be so reflective of the Devolving Culture. The screenplay was cleverly written without moralizing any behavior. The parents, her father and step mother, were initially detached and disengaged. They loved her and were disappointed of course, but couldn't judge her. After all, kids have sex and she just happened to be unlucky enough to get pregnant. She was going to have an abortion but changed her mind, not because abortion is wrong or anything, but because she learned that the fetus has fingernails. It was HER DECISION TO MAKE. Her friend helped her look for adoptive parents, she agreed to give the baby to them and then we watched her go through nine months of attending school and her normal activities until the baby was born. The ending has a twist of course. Nothing in life turns out quite like you expect, accept true love, which is what this young girl and her boyfriend learned they have in the end. (I think I want to puke!) I felt so sorry for that poor girl. She had no spiritual input. No priest. No minister. Not even her own parents guided her through deep questions she must have had about her raging hormones. Her father gave her no boundaries and set no example of what a protector should be. She would be scarred for life. She would live with the consequences of her actions forever. Although I applaud the fact that she did not abort the baby, it was appalling to me to suggest that it would have been OK if she did. She would have lived with that scar for the rest of her life as well. I couldn't help but look at this young girl's future. Without Jesus Christ and a radical change in her life, she would sadly grow up and see the same patterns of moral decline repeated in her own children, only with each successive generation the decline increases. Alas, it was only a movie, but so real and this scenario is being played out in home after home.

Alcohol consumption and drug abuse are now at epidemic levels. The social stigma against drinking has all but been erased. There was a time when abstainers were viewed as honorable people, but now are depicted as socially backward. Alcohol and drugs are readily available to our children. If they don't sneak it, some parents buy it for them, rationalizing that they are going to drink anyway. They would have them drink in their home rather than out on the street or somewhere they could get hurt or hurt someone else. Note in most states it is against the law to provide alcohol to minors. How many accidents could have been prevented if substances were not involved? How many marriages would still be intact if not for substance abuse? How many families would still be together if not for substance abuse? How many people would still be alive today if not for substance abuse?

Tabloid newsprints and television shows thrive on reporting the latest scandals of the famous and infamous. A lot of money is made from sensationalizing the troubled lives of alcoholic/drug addicted, partying, out of control starlets and athletes who have also made copious amounts of money and are not handling the newfound fortune and fame well. These reported escapades become more disgusting with each new revelation. It's all about money. The public is buying and they are selling. And then we wonder why there is suddenly a barrage of teachers having sex with young students, not just male teachers with female students, but female teachers having sex with young male students. Without overstating the obvious, children and adults are inundated with violent, bloody, murderous acts which have become much too commonplace in our media. No, we are not growing as a society, we are digressing. We are slipping further and further into the abyss of spiritual, moral and social decay.

Perilous Times

Just a few years after Christ's resurrection, Paul the Apostle wrote a letter to his protégé, Timothy, who was the pastor of a thriving church in the City of Ephesus. Ephesus was a seaport with a bustling economy and a very diverse population. The church was growing successfully in a culturally corrupt community of many philosophical ideas and religions. In order to prepare Timothy for his role as a pastor, Paul wrote about the cultural conditions that he believed would occur in the last days. To be sure, Paul and Timothy thought they were living in the last days and would, themselves, see these predictions come to fruition, and to some extent did, but they are ever more relevant in light of current conditions.

*BUT UNDERSTAND this, that **in the last days** will come (set in)perilous times of great stress and trouble [hard to deal with and hard to bear]. v.2*

*For people will be lovers of self and [utterly] **self-centered, lovers of money** and aroused by an inordinate [greedy] desire for wealth, proud and arrogant and contemptuous boasters. They will be abusive (**blasphemous,** scoffing), **disobedient to parents,** ungrateful, unholy and profane. v.3*

*[They will be] **without natural [human] affection** (callous and inhuman), relentless (admitting of no truce or appeasement); [they will be] **slanderers** (false accusers, troublemakers), intemperate and **loose in morals** and conduct, uncontrolled and fierce, haters of good. v.4*

*[They will be] treacherous [**betrayers**], rash, [and] inflated with self-conceit. [They will be] **lovers of sensual pleasures** and vain amusements more than and **rather than lovers of God.** v.5*

For [although] they hold a form of piety (true religion), they deny and reject and are strangers to the power of it [their conduct belies the genuineness of their profession]. Avoid [all] such people[turn away from them].

2 Timothy 3:1-5 AMP

The King James Version of the Bible says they have a "form of godliness" but deny "the power thereof." Nonetheless, the Prophet Isaiah assured us that as darkness would increase so would the light. It certainly is dark out there for us as Christians and this generation, but the Light of God is shining brighter and brighter. Don't lose hope. It ain't over till the fat lady sings and she's just doing her vocal warm up exercises. Christ is the Morning Star and He resides in us shining through us. He is the Hope of Glory. The Apostle Peter gave us further hope when he said,

*And we have the prophetic word [made] firmer still. You will do well to pay close attention to it as to a lamp shining in a dismal (squalid and dark) place, **until the day breaks through [the gloom]** and **the Morning Star rises** (comes into being) in your hearts.*

2 Peter 1:19 AMP

The roots were evident in Timothy's city and the roots are still here today. The roots are a sickness, an invasive, oppressive disease that is destroying us. The roots must be addressed. We have to get to the cancerous roots that are eating away our organs. To be sure spiritual chemotherapy and radiation treatments are needed, but more importantly, there has to be a cure. Before there is a cure you have to determine the cause. Holistic

medicine focuses on finding the cause and then prevention of the disease, by eating right, not smoking or ingesting other harmful chemicals, getting the proper exercise and having a healthy spiritual life. The holistic approach focuses on the whole man-spiritually, socially, mentally, physically and financially. Let's take that approach. How did we get here? What is the cause of this serious culture crisis?

CHAPTER FIVE

Getting to the Cause

Thank God for modern medical science and technology. Without the discovery of antibiotics and other medicines and procedures surely many millions of lives would be lost. By learning that a certain virus is the cause of an illness the appropriate medication or immunization could be applied. Illnesses that once wiped out whole communities are now all but annihilated. It has taken researchers to find the cause in order to bring the cure. Likewise, we must find what is causing the root problems of the Devolving Culture.

To do that, we have to go back all the way to the beginning and we must use the Holy Bible as our resource. Now I realize that the current cultural climate does not necessarily accept the Bible as being infallible, but that argument flies in the face of what the Bible says of itself... *All scripture is given by inspiration of God, and is profitable for doctrine, for reproof, for correction, for instruction in righteousness...* 2 Timothy 3:16 KJV

ALL scripture, not parts of it or our favorite part of it, but ALL scripture is given by inspiration of God to MEN. Yes, men are fallible, but that is the beauty of the Word of God. These inspired writings were given to many different individuals over a 1500 year span and every word dictated lines up with one another without contradiction. The most unique book of life was written for one main reason—the redemption of mankind. It has survived persecution, been banned, burned and outlawed. No one book has had as much harsh criticism, venom, skepticism, or hammering away at its veracity. No other religion or mindset can match its accuracy of prophesies or history. Christ Himself came to earth fulfilling the Bible's prophetic utterances. His birth, his ministry, his death and resurrection were foretold thousands of years before. Acts 1:3 KJV states, *To whom also he shewed himself alive after his passion by many infallible proofs, being seen of them forty days, and speaking of the things pertaining to the kingdom of God.* His followers had many infallible proofs and were convinced that God had raised Him from the dead because they ate with Him, spoke with Him, and lived with Him for days afterward. They were willing to die for this belief and many did, rather than deny the Savior who had given His life for them.

Why Christ?

Why was it necessary for Jesus to give His life? Again, we have to go back to the beginning. The very first book of the Bible, Genesis, gives the account of God desiring to have fellowship with a family. This story is not a fairy tale, but a true account of God's creation. So many people dismiss it trying to rationalize how many days/years it took to create the earth and that evolution would have taken millions of years. Divorce yourself from the timeline for a moment and comprehend what God actually did.

Prior to creation God had a Son and His Holy Spirit but the angels were servants, not family. God wanted to expand his family and so created a world for that family to live in then created the race of MAN, male and female.[11] Their world or garden was a perfect atmosphere with abundance of anything and everything they could desire. God walked with them in the cool of the day. He had fellowship with his family who would reproduce and replenish the garden to fill and expand over the entire earth. (Many scholars attribute the geographical area of the Garden of Eden to being in modern day Iraq, the cradle of civilization.) Adam and Eve were made in the likeness and image of God. They were not servants, unlike their tempter, Lucifer, who was a fallen angel.[12]

The Bible tells how Satan, or Lucifer, who was a prince of angels, made a conscious decision that he wanted to be equal with God, rebelled and even convinced a third of the angelic hosts to join him in warfare against God.[13] In that moment, the devil became SIN, which literally means rebellion against God. Iniquity was found in him. Jesus relays the account to his followers telling them He witnessed Satan being thrown out of heaven.[14] Many say that is when darkness appeared on the earth, when the fallen angel, the devil, invaded earth's planet. He was now

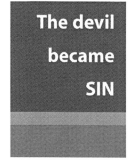

The devil became SIN

extremely jealous of this new MAN who had all the rights and privileges with God he so desired for himself. He tempted the woman by convincing her to eat of the one tree in the center of the garden, the tree of the knowledge of good and evil, which was God's property. Adam and Eve had been warned not to eat of it or suffer death. Of course, the enemy lied to Eve and told her she would not die but instead be like God. It was all a lie. Physical death for them, as it turned out, would take hundreds of years, but spiritual death, spiritual separation from the Creator, happened immediately. The irony is that Adam and Eve were already like God, being born into the God class, the family of God. They didn't need to eat the fruit to discover they were already created in His likeness and image.

One tragic decision

The greatest human tragedy in this story is that, though Eve was deceived, Adam was not. He understood the magnitude of his actions and deliberately participated. He was not away somewhere else in the Garden, while Lucifer tempted Eve. He was standing right beside her. Eve handed him the fruit, he ate of it and in that moment committed high treason against Almighty God. In one tragic decision Adam gave his God given authority to the betrayer who now could rule over the MAN, the family, God loved so much. SIN and its curse — spiritual and natural death — now had control over the earth and the results of the curse of sin were unleashed — sickness, disease, poverty, lack, destruction and evil of every kind.

God immediately put a plan in motion to send His Son, Jesus, to redeem MAN from SIN and its curse. The historical events of the Nation of Israel outlined in the scriptures depict a people and a world increasingly dominated by vile, grotesque behavior. Violence and every form of evil were unleashed. Even the leaders that God ordained could not rescue humankind from their own destruction. God's great love demanded that Jesus would be born to a humble Jewish girl, a virgin, who conceived by the Holy Spirit. All of this was prophesied and written by the prophets. The Bible says that Jesus was obedient to the heavenly calling.[15] His mission was accomplished. Not only did He perform great miracles with signs and wonders in His earthly ministry, but He willingly and innocently went to the cross, suffering indescribable torture and pain. Christ paid the penalty of MAN's betrayal. He took MAN's place. He became SIN, went into the dominion of hell, faced Satan and took back MAN's authority.[16]

> **Christ paid the penalty**

One of those proverbial "why God" questions is, if God is Omniscient, all knowing and all seeing, why did He create man knowing that man would sin against Him? The Bible tells us that God, *Who is and Who was and Who is to come* (Revelation 1:4 AMP) does not and has never operated in the realm of "time." Time was manifest when MAN committed SIN. We are living in a period of "time" generated by the fall of man. According to the Bible, when this current age has ended time will be no more. (Rev. 10:6 KJV) Yes, God knew that man would sin and He had a plan already in place to bring the cure. Jesus, God's Son, accepted the plan before time began, before the foundation of the world. (Ephesians 1:4 and 1 Peter 1:20 KJV) In the Book of Revelation, John the Apostle saw the Redeemer saying, *I am the Alpha and the Omega, the Beginning and the End, says the Lord God, He Who is and Who was and Who is to come, the Almighty (the Ruler of all).* (Revelation 1:8 AMP) God looked into the future and saw YOU and me. Jesus was willing to give His life for YOU and me. He knew what was ahead and thought YOU and I were worth the price.

The Followers' Assignment

Jesus' followers saw and lived with a resurrected Christ. Christ is not Jesus' last name. Christ means the Anointed Messiah, the promised One who came to remove burdens and destroy yokes of bondage. He gave instructions to go into all the world and preach this truth—the Gospel—that we must receive Him and be born again, from death to life, from sin to redemption, from sickness to health, from poverty to blessing.[17] They were committed to the message as they watched their risen Savior ascend into the heavens and disappear before their very eyes. He told them He would return for them and the family His Father loved so deeply. That is the hope that Christians of every denomination still have. That is the message Christians still believe and preach—that you don't have to be controlled by SIN and its consequences, but you can live free and receive eternal life here on this earth and in heaven with Christ.

46

The alternative is to continue to be dominated by Satan, hanging on to SIN and its results, and to live forever in hell with the great deceiver. Oh no. Here we go. You see many just cannot accept that there is a heaven and a hell. Some believe there is a heaven and as long as they are a good person they will certainly go there, but they don't believe in hell. How could a loving God send people to a terrible place like hell? The truth is God isn't sending anyone to hell. He created hell for Satan and the fallen angels. We send ourselves to hell by refusing to accept God's redemption. And there's that word. SIN! The cultural community does not want to acknowledge that wrong behavior is indeed sin. People will justify their actions with excuse after excuse, but when you boil it all down the cause of our morality breakdown is sin, rebellion against God. John the Beloved told us,

> *For God so greatly loved and dearly prized the world that He [even] gave up His only begotten (unique) Son, so that whoever* **believes** *in (trusts in, clings to, relies on) Him* **shall not perish** *(come to destruction, be lost) but have eternal (everlasting) life.* **For God did not send the Son into the world in order to judge** *(to reject, to condemn, to pass sentence on) the world,* **but that the world might find salvation** *and be made safe and sound* **through Him.**
>
> John 3:16, 17 AMP

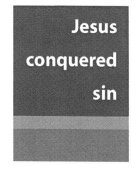

Sin has been a reality since Satan rebelled. The good news is that Jesus Christ conquered sin. It is possible to live above sin and its repercussions. The Message Bible says, *I write this, dear children, to guide you out of sin. But if anyone does sin, we have a Priest-Friend in the presence of the Father: Jesus Christ, righteous Jesus. When he served as a sacrifice for our sins, he solved the sin problem for good—not only ours, but the whole world's. Here's how we can be sure that we know God in the right way: Keep his commandments.* 1 John 2:1-3

Keep His commandments. Believe God and do what God says. God tells us His will through His Word and the church of Jesus Christ, the family of God, exists to help a dying world know the cause of their behavior and that there is a way out of their sin. You might suggest that society, historically, has been full of debauchery and that the Christian church has not always represented the highest of standards. That would be true. There are moments in history the church cannot be proud of. Sadly, the Devolving Culture has continued to infiltrate God's own family on this earth and it appears now, as Phil Cooke penned, "…that Oprah is America's pastor, the vestments of the twenty-first-century church are manufactured by Nike, the communion table is poured by a barista from Starbucks, and… people confess their sins on daytime television…"[18] I would like to examine some of that evidence.

CHAPTER SIX

The Secret Revealed

Worldwide Christian church growth is phenomenal. Third world countries are exploding with thousands attending church services from the jungles of Africa to the former Soviet Union. Arguably the largest church in the world boasts almost one million members in Seoul, Korea. Missionaries tell us they are having their greatest impact in Muslim nations with multiplied thousands converting to Christianity. The Gospel message is having tremendous success across our globe. Contrast that with the empty cathedrals in Europe and across America. What's wrong? The Devolving Culture would suggest that Europeans and Americans are now too educated and enlightened to accept antiquated Christian doctrines. Some Christians in established faiths have been negatively influenced and have fallen prey to what the Bible calls a "great falling away."[19]

The Bible says that in the last days people would be easily deceived and succumb to "seducing spirits."[20] A seducing spirit is one that leads away from established truth. The chief seducer is the enemy of our faith—Satan. He is the thief that comes to steal, kill and destroy. (John 10:10 KJV) That is the devil's job description. That is what he did to Adam and Eve in the Garden. He deceived them and stole their God-given authority. His lies initiated death and its consequences and destroyed the fellowship they had with Father God. He stole from them, he killed them and destroyed them.

Here we go. I know that many people do not believe in a literal devil and that is part of his deception. That is the great lie. In truth evil is present in this world in a persona called Satan and he has many fallen angels, demonic beings, who roam this earth, *seeking whom he may devour* (1 Peter 5:8 KJV). Demonic forces continue to work through human beings using the same methods of deception—stealing, killing, and destroying. These same demonic forces inspire humans to promote false teachings and ideas that steer people away from the Truth (John 10:10).

One such demonically inspired teaching, which has been promoted on the *Oprah Winfrey Show* and in her magazine, is called "The Secret." "The Secret" has been embraced by metaphysical philosophers and others in the New Age Movement as being one of the most phenomenal revelations of the 21st Century. Millions of people are being drawn to this doctrine, giving testimonials of true love found, financial increase, peace, prosperity and real joy for the first time in their lives. It is purported to be the secret to life. At first glance one might think what could possibly be wrong with such a positive outlook on life?

The New Age doctrine of "The Secret," in the opinion of most Christian theologians and church leaders, is a lie. It is a false, anti-Christ doctrine, and it is dangerous for Christians to blindly hear and receive the beliefs of those involved in such metaphysical concepts. Skepticism of "The Secret" is not just relegated to those of the Christian faith. Peter Birkenhead of *salon.com* wrote an article entitled, "Oprah's ugly secret." He states, "...what really makes "The Secret" more than a variation on an old theme is the involvement of Oprah Winfrey, who lends the whole enterprise more prestige, and, because of that prestige, more venality, than any previous self-help scam. Oprah hasn't just endorsed "The Secret"; she's championed it, put herself at the apex of its pyramid, and helped create a symbiotic economy of New Age quacks..."[21]

By giving heed to these deceptions, even when they are given credibility by popular and well meaning personalities, you set yourself up. The devil will insure a slow erosion of your convictions and cause you to begin questioning sacred truths of God's Word. That is the method he used in the Garden. We must be well educated, armed with correct information and with God-given tools to combat the great deceiver.

Where Did it Come From?

At the end of 2004, its founder, Rhonda Byrne, was in a difficult time in her life and came across a book over 100 years old entitled, *The Science of Getting Rich*, by Wallace Wattles.[22] Reading that book took her on a journey of researching various world religions and teachings. She says there was a common

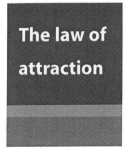

The law of attraction

thread of truth at the core of each of these which results in the law that governs the universe—the law that generates success and happiness—the law of attraction. According to Ms. Byrne and apparently millions more who agree with her, "...without exception, every human being has the ability to transform any weakness or suffering into strength, power, perfect peace, health, and abundance."[23] The law is defined as; human beings attract positive or negative energy to their lives by intentionally willing and/or speaking it into being. Many in the movement will even quote Christ's teachings as one of their resources. Rhonda Byrne's research became a best selling video and a book and has spawned a plethora of subsequent collaborating books by other authors.

This freshly articulated doctrine is indicative of what I have termed the Devolving Culture, which states there is truth in all beliefs that all opinions are equal; open minded tolerant people should drop their negative views of other religions and spiritual pursuits and accept the validity of the underlying truth in each. The problem with this wave of false doctrine is that Christ is not ONE of the ways in the law of attraction. He is THE WAY.

Jesus said to him, I am the Way and the Truth and the Life; no one comes to the Father except by (through) Me.

John 14:6 AMP

"The Secret" ideology also gives all the power to humankind; each individual is in control of his/her own destiny simply by utilizing this power of attraction. I am not denying that the law works. The principle certainly works because it is the Word of God. Jesus taught this law and that we receive its power from Jehovah God and His Word. We don't have the power within our own human nature. The power comes from God, not some

The power comes from God

abstract entity somewhere in the universe. "The Secret" leaves people, *Having a form of godliness, but denying the power thereof: from such turn away.* 2 Timothy 3:5

As a pastor, I am concerned that some who have not attended church in years or perhaps have never attended and have had no biblical teaching will see this video or read the book and think, *This is the answer I have been looking for.* Or perhaps a well meaning Christian who isn't very knowledgeable in the scriptures would say, *That sounds like what my pastor says.* The difficulty is that it is similar to Christian doctrines, because it extracts truth from the scriptures, while also fusing Bible reality into other metaphysical philosophies. Let me give some examples of catch phrases used by "The Secret" followers and how they compare to scripture:

The Secret	The Holy Bible
Life Coaches	*And he gave some, apostles; and some, prophets; and some, evangelists; and some, pastors and teachers; For the perfecting of the saints, for the work of the ministry, for the edifying of the body of Christ:* Ephesians 4:11,12 KJV

Law of Attraction

Positive or negative thinking brings the reality into
your life. (Feelings are
magnets to bring things
from the universe.)

*For as he thinks in his heart,
so is he.*
Proverbs 23:7 KJV

*For this reason I am telling you,
whatever you ask for in prayer,
believe (trust and be confident)
that it is granted to you, and you
will [get it].* Mark 11:24 AMP

Stepping out in faith to sow
thought seeds.

*Do not be deceived and deluded
and misled; God will not allow
Himself to be sneered at (scorned,
disdained, or mocked by mere
pretensions or professions, or by
His precepts being set aside.) [He
inevitably deludes himself who
attempts to delude God.] For whatever a man sows, that and that
only is what he will reap.*
Galatians 6:7 AMP

Speaking positive words brings
the reality in your life.

*And Jesus, replying, said to them,
Have faith in God [constantly].
Truly I tell you, whoever says to
this mountain, Be lifted up and
thrown into the sea! and does not
doubt at all in his heart but believes
that what he says will take place, it
will be done for him. For this reason
I am telling you, whatever you ask
for in prayer, believe (trust and be
confident) that it is granted to you,
and you will [get it]. Reality into
your life.* Mark 11:22-24 AMP

Visioneering/Vision Board

And the Lord answered me and said, Write the vision and engrave it so plainly upon tablets that everyone who passes may [be able to] read [it easily and quickly] as he hastens by. For the vision is yet for an appointed time and it hastens to the end [fulfillment]; it will not deceive or disappoint. Though it tarry, wait [earnestly] for it, because it will surely come; it will not be behindhand on its appointed day. Habakkuk 2:2,3 AMP

Faith is believing in the Universal Law of Attraction.

And Jesus, replying, said to them, Have faith in God[constantly]. Mark 11:22 AMP

NOW FAITH is the assurance (the confirmation, the title deed) of the things [we] hope for, being the proof of things [we] do not see and the conviction of their reality [faith perceiving as real fact what is not revealed to the senses].

For by [faith—trust and holy fervor born of faith] the men of old had divine testimony borne to them and obtained a good report. Hebrews 11:1,2 AMP

Life Coaches of "The Secret" teach followers that you can bring positive energy from the universe into your life by thinking, believing, and speaking it. They refer to it in mysterious, mystical terms. Christianity teaches that if we believe in our heart and say it with our mouth we will be saved from sin, and we can have those things that we desire when we pray. (Romans 10:8-10 and Mark 11:24 KJV) Life Coaches teach how to go from shallowness, or what Christians know as unbelief, to your "core of peace." Of course, the only real peace or assurance a person can have is through salvation in Jesus Christ. The Word of God tells us that man is a spirit being who possesses a soul (mind, will and emotions) and who lives in a human body. The spirit is the real YOU. The spirit is where Christ resides when we invite Him into our hearts. We begin then to renew our soul (our mind, will and emotions) to be conformed to His way of doing things. It is our flesh that will die one day, but the real US, our spirit man, will live forever.

No New Revelation

The mysticism behind "The Secret" actually is not a sudden new revelation. The ideology and spirit have been prevalent in pagan and heathen religions for centuries. It is a deception. In fact, the leaders of the early church faced this philosophy. Paul wrote about it in his New Testament letters to the various churches as did the Apostles Peter and John. Two similar doctrines in contradiction to the Gospel message were espoused by the Gnostics and the Antimonians.

The word gnosis means knowledge. Gnosticism has many varying beliefs, but generally states that certain people are given knowledge of a higher being. Gnostics of the New Testament received the teachings of Jesus, but did not receive Him as the Son of God. They believed in esoteric knowledge that gave them special access to the transcendent being. These Gnostics believed they were a select group of insiders who had mystical insight of the universe that others did not have. In other words, they knew the secret to the mysteries of life.

The Antimonians believed in salvation through Jesus Christ but twisted God's grace by teaching that salvation was by grace alone, therefore moral law was irrelevant. On this premise as long as you believed in God you could define your own morality. You could live any way you pleased. The Antimonians therefore lived a very licentious lifestyle. They acted no differently than those in pagan religions who used sex and sexual perversion as a means of worship in their temples, only to the Antimonian it was all about their own pleasure and desires. Antimonians were convinced they were spiritually correct and should not be judged for their conduct. The early church leaders vehemently preached against these false doctrines and stressed sexual conduct as outlined in the scriptures.

I see these ancient doctrines incorporated in "The Secret." Proponents of "The Secret" place MAN and his special knowledge at the center of the universe. They draw moral conduct from multiple sources. There is no one standard code of morality, because what may be right for one person is not necessarily right for another. Whatever religion or spiritual teaching you draw from is fine since the law of attraction is the common thread in all. They believe they have uncovered a mystical revelation, which they are happy to share with you via the sale of their DVDSs and books. These products have made many very wealthy indeed.

In his book, *Culturally Incorrect,* Rod Parsley outlines another modern doctrine that I believe also traces its spiritual roots to these ancient beliefs. Pastor Parsley discuses Monism/Pantheism which means that everything is God and God is in everything. Pantheism actually states that there are multiple gods. "All matter energy, spirit, and everything composed of these elements are simply part of a cosmic Oneness."[24] This thinking is the basis of much of the current New Age philosophies, which I believe includes the teachings of "The Secret." The universe as they put it is that cosmic oneness. In the last chapter of this book, I will discuss another New Age doctrine, in addition to "The Secret," even more alarming, to which Oprah Winfrey has given voice. The mindset of New Age teachings is a diabolical deception that does not conform to the teachings of the Holy Bible. While certain catch phrases of "The Secret" may sound eerily similar to Christian teachings, they derive from totally different sources. One is from God and one is demonically inspired.

It is imperative that believing Believers discern the differences. Peter wrote letters to his fellow Christians, referring to the cult doctrines of the Gnostics and the Antimonians, saying we have been given "exceeding great and precious promises" so that we can escape "the corruption that is in the world through lust." (2 Peter 1:4 KJV) God has not abandoned us to find our own way through the confusion and madness of a lost world. He has given us His Word to guide us, pastors and teachers to instruct us and the fellowship of other Believers to encourage us on our journey.

The Secret Place

You do not need a spiritual guru to reveal the secret of the universe. In fact it's not a secret anymore and hasn't been a secret for over 2,000 years. The mystery was hidden in Christ from God's enemy (1 Corinthians 2:8). The Holy Bible tells us plainly that the mystery has been revealed now to those "adopted" into the family of God, i.e., born again Christians. Paul wrote to his son in the faith, Timothy, who was the pastor at the church in Ephesus,

> *To the praise of the glory of his grace, wherein he hath made us accepted in the beloved. In whom we have redemption through his blood, the forgiveness of sins, according to the riches of his grace; Wherein he hath abounded toward us in all wisdom and prudence;* **Having made known unto us the mystery** *of his will, according to his good pleasure which he hath purposed in himself:*
>
> Ephesians 1:6-9 KJV

Paul states that we have been accepted in the beloved, which is King James dialogue for being a part of the family of

THE OPRAHFICATION OF OUR CULTURE

God through the blood of Jesus Christ. Those of us in the family of God have been given the secret to the mystery. Of course, you can live an abundant, prosperous, healthy life because of what Jesus accomplished through His passion, through his suffering on the cross and through His resurrection. The Greek word "sozo"[25] meaning salvation describes total salvation for the whole man—deliverance from sin, sickness, poverty. We can be born again and have real life in God spiritually, mentally, physically, socially and financially. Yes, the secret has been revealed through the Word of God.

Psalm 25:14	*The **secret** of the LORD is with them that fear him; and he will shew them his covenant.*
Psalm 91:1, 2	*He that dwelleth in the **secret** place of the most High shall abide under the shadow of the Almighty. I will say of the LORD, He is my refuge and my fortress: my God; in him will I trust.*
Proverbs 3:32	*For the froward is abomination to the LORD: but his **secret** is with the righteous.*
Matthew 13:34, 35	*All **these things spake Jesus** unto the multitude in parables; and without a parable spake he not unto them: That it might be fulfilled which was spoken by the prophet, saying, I will open my mouth in parables; **I will utter things***

which have been kept secret from the foundation of the world.

Luke 8:17

For **nothing is secret,** *that shall not be made manifest; neither any thing hid, that shall not be known and come abroad.*

Romans 16:25, 26

Now to him that is of power to stablish you according to my gospel, and the preaching of Jesus Christ, according to **the revelation of the mystery, which was kept secret since the world began, But now is made manifest,** *and by the scriptures of the prophets, according to the commandment of the everlasting God, made known to all nations for the obedience of faith:*

CHAPTER SEVEN

The *Un*Cultured Church

In the midst of screaming spiritual nonsense believers can still assemble together in the construct of the church and be rejuvenated to go back out and face down the lies of the enemy. Yes, the current culture doesn't put much credence in church attendance, but to a Christian the church is our ark of safety. Paul told the church at Rome,

> And let us consider and give attentive, continuous care to watching over one another, studying how we may stir up (stimulate and incite) to love and helpful deeds and noble activities, **Not forsaking or neglecting to assemble together [as believers]**, as is the habit of some people, but admonishing (warning, urging, and encouraging) one another, and all the more faithfully as you see the day approaching.
>
> Hebrews 10:24,25 AMP

Church attendance is more relevant today than ever as we see "the day approaching," the soon returning of our Lord and Savior Jesus Christ. As we anticipate Christ's return, we must get our spiritual houses in order, corporately and personally.

We have some work to do. We must work untiringly to get the Devolving Culture out of the church.

The *Un*Cultured church in my definition would be one that is unencumbered by corrupt moral standards of the day. I refer to the church as un-cultured, because according to one definition the word culture means; a particular society at a particular time and place.[26] The church should not be defined by this particular current society. The *Un*Cultured church should be principled by Godly standards, not by those of television personalities, movie stars and educated non-Christian ideologues. I have heard it said that some people are educated far beyond their intellect. This is certainly accurate of some in the New Age Movement. They become so esoteric that they no longer have common sense. Common sense ain't so common any more. Here's what the Message Bible says of the church:

> *The church, you see, is not peripheral to the world; the world is peripheral to the church. The church is Christ's body, in which he speaks and acts, by which he fills everything with his presence.*

> Ephesians 1:23

God has a standard

The church, the Body of Christ, should not and is not standing on the sidelines waiting for our culture to dictate standards. The church is the voice to our world that God has a standard. Is it idealistic to expect an *Un*Cultured Church in today's world? We are told in God's Word that He is returning for a glorious church.[27] That must mean that He expects us to live in this society without being influenced by it. However, pastors today are being pressured to fill empty seats by ignoring people's lifestyles and overlooking their immoral behavior. Many pastors focus on positive issues that evoke good feelings and compromise spiritual integrity for forms of entertainment. Entertainment in and of itself is fine as long it uses the power of the Holy Spirit to bring people to the Gospel message and make disciples of them, however when a positive message and the tools of media and arts are utilized purely to attract a crowd it leaves people empty and shallow.

The 20,000 member Willow Creek Community Church in Illinois popularized the seeker sensitive approach, which presents a more casual, relaxed atmosphere than formal traditional services and uses all the modern methods of communication. The pastor of Willow Creek recently made a startling admission. "We made a mistake," Bill Hybels told more than 80,000 church leaders participating in an August Willow Creek Association conference. "When people crossed the line of faith and became Christians, we should have started telling people and teaching people that they have to take responsibility to become 'self-feeders.'"[28]

In a 2003 survey the church discovered that, "nearly one out of every four people at Willow Creek were stalled in their spiritual growth or dissatisfied with the church—and many of them were considering leaving."[29] That speaks volumes. People ARE spiritually hungry for discipleship. Millions of people around the world ARE being attracted to spiritual teachings such as "The Secret" and they are attracted to the church as well, but we have to help them become true

Believers and followers. We can utilize modern tools and still keep the integrity of the Word intact and the move of the Holy Spirit in our services. The *Un*Cultured Church should remain relevant to the Devolving Culture without adopting its standards.

It is possible for the church to abide by a higher standard and even affect the negative world around us, yet too often the church deals with the same raw issues facing society. Divorce rates are said to be as high among Christians as non Christians. Churches are filled with people who have chemical addictions and sexual addictions. Pornography is rampant and easily accessible to both men and women via the internet. Every day the church world hears new stories of lying, stealing, cheating, backbiting, betrayal, and corruption by the clergy and congregant alike.

Financial and sexual corruption is certainly not anything extraordinary in today's society, and it is just as prevalent in the church. My husband and I have been in the ministry over thirty years and have seen and heard many disappointing accounts of moral failures. Never in our lives, though, have we witnessed such complacency, lack of conviction and callousness of heart. You've heard the stories as well. The national news media, ever hungry for higher ratings, is all too eager to sensationalize the "fall" of what they term "televangelists." Perhaps you have been a member of a congregation where leadership failed. Wherever there are imperfect people there is imperfect behavior, including inside the church.

Every Evil Work

Steve and I learned years ago, though, that the number one thing destroying any work, whether it be religious, business, marital or otherwise is STRIFE! James 3:16 says, *For where envying and strife is, there is confusion and every evil work.* Evil is still in this world. Demons love to hang out in governments, businesses, marriages and families to cause division. Again, the job description of the enemy is to steal, kill and destroy. He'll tear apart any relationship in order to achieve his objective, especially if that entity is doing a great work for God. Oh, yes. Satan hangs out in churches. The devil will use anyone to stir up strife whether they realize they are being used or not.

John Hagee, Pastor of Cornerstone Church in San Antonio, Texas, once stated on his television broadcast that some members of churches are meaner than members of the mob. The mafia operates by a long traditional code of covenant. Members take care of one another. Breaking that covenant insures your demise. In an odd sort of way, it would be great if more church members could fully understand the concept of that covenant relationship. Christians should be unwilling to break that code, but so many do. Consequently, in an environment where one would expect the love of God to be prevalent, church members can often be the cruelest folks — gossiping, tale bearing, slandering. Many carry the mindset of the world right into the church pew.

Imperfect people imperfect behavior

Pastors have a daunting assignment. It is the responsibility of a pastor to guide, guard and govern the members of a church, teaching them how to live above their imperfections, in an imperfect world. Many charismatic leaders can draw a crowd, but a pastor will make disciples. Most times that is appreciated, but often it is not. I don't know of a pastor who has not experienced what we term the "Absalom spirit."

The Old Testament tells the story of King David's own son, Absalom, who had been offended unknowingly by his father. Absalom betrayed David, and tried to displace his father from the throne in order to make himself king instead. His effort failed and Absalom was killed in the battle. Like Absalom, too often people mistake the spiritual correction of their pastor as a form of rejection and then respond with the same type of action that Absalom took. People betray their leader by causing an insurrection and defection. They gather others to their "cause," which is their offence, and persuade them to abandon discipleship. Sometimes these defections occur in the corporate world through dissolving of business partnerships, in families through divorce and family schisms and even church splits, which are heartbreaking for everyone involved. My husband and I have certainly not been immune. I tease him all the time that he has become a bishop by default as people leave and start their own "goat gatherings."

However, in the last several years we have noticed a much higher level of ungodliness and a degree of impurity in these "insurrections" that is parallel to what is being demonstrated in the current culture. When my husband and I obeyed the call to pastor, we never imagined some of the difficult challenges we would face, because of the culture in which we live. I give these following examples, only to highlight the magnitude of moral dereliction existing in churches. I believe corruption in the house of God is in direct correlation to what I have termed the Devolving Culture, which again is; everyone is responsible for his/her own moral compass and should not be judged; all opinions are equal. In each of these following cases, the defectors believed they were in the right and were above correction.

One of the Kids

The first example may seem, at first glance, not to be quite so ominous, but a deeper examination reveals serious implications. It is of a young married couple we were excited to mentor in the early days of our church. Their heart's desire was for teenagers and we ordained them as our youth pastors. The husband went through our school of ministry, studying Bible teachings, ministerial ethics, and protocol. We personally tutored them in "avoiding the appearance of evil"[30] by having a guideline of conduct with children. They were told not to become "buddies" with the kids. They were always to act as the adult making sure the children had clear boundaries of respect and authority. The youth meetings were to be conducted at the church and never in their home. However, we learned that they were bringing in teenagers to "baby sit" their own small children which turned into socializing at the youth pastor's home. They would take kids with them to hang out at the mall and it was difficult to distinguish the husband, particularly, from the other teenagers.

When we addressed this with the couple they assured us they would cease all such activity. We told them that if we ever saw any hint of flirtation or behavior that could even be suggested improper they would be dismissed immediately. Some time later I happened to be driving up to the church and I saw the young man standing out front with one of the teenage girls. Their backs were to me so they didn't notice my approach. He was holding her hand, putting his arm around her, putting his face close to hers, as if they were boyfriend and girlfriend. Needless to say, the couple's employment with the church was terminated, which caused hurt feelings with some teenagers and their families who did not know of the details of their dismissal. Some families left our church and blamed us, the pastors, for firing that couple "unfairly" in their words. My husband and I were determined to respect this young man and his family's privacy by not communicating the reasons of their departure with other church members. We later learned that they had severely bad mouthed our ministry and had gathered a small company of disgruntled families who were all of like minds against "those pastors."

What if we had let that flirtatious irresponsible behavior continue? Where could that have led? What is the logical conclusion? The obvious would be sexual advances on the young girl and many lives destroyed. However, the story communicated from the youth pastors and their family and friends was that the pastors were unfair and uncaring, when in reality the pastors saved that young girl and the youth pastor from certain heartache. The Devolving Culture would have made excuses for the youth pastor's behavior. That mindset would rationalize that he had a minor innocent indiscretion and after all was doing such a good job and working so hard that the pastors should have been more tolerant and understanding and forgiving. Forgiveness is fine but allowing wrong behavior in the church is not.

The Children's Pastors From Hell

The second example is more sobering. Several years ago we were in dire need of a children's pastor. I pursued all the usual avenues for job placement at Christian colleges and other ministries receiving a stack of resumes. After interviewing a host of prospective ministers, I hired a couple with a young family on a trial basis. I spoke with the head of their licensing organization who assured me that if there was any difficulty he would personally be available to intervene. That wisdom later proved to be invaluable. You see, sometimes you prepare and make decisions you believe will be successful, but the enemy comes in to disrupt and destroy and this was one of those times.

Not long after their temporary hiring, we learned a fact that was not included in their resume. The couple had been pastors of a small church where the husband had been sexually involved with another woman. Strong spiritual oversight and counseling had saved their marriage, but they had resigned from the church. When confronted with this new found information, the husband promised that he had learned from his past failure. He hoped he and his wife could set an example to help other couples with similar problems receive restoration. He asked us to give him grace. Steve and I were once again faced with a pastor's heart of seeing the potential. We wanted to believe that this would all work out fine, but an administrator would have probably fired him on the spot. We agreed to allow his trial employment to continue knowing that his licensor had promised to assist us with any difficulty should it arise.

Soon parents were complaining to us that the children of this couple were undisciplined and unmannerly and usually looked unkempt. We heard reports of screaming matches between the husband and wife, where the husband would openly berate his wife. Other leaders in our church conveyed how this man attacked them verbally in a public hotel. We had already decided to release them when we received even more alarming news. Parents called asking if we had endorsed a children's church co-ed "sleep over" at the children's pastors' home. Outraged parents told us their children had been invited by this couple, but their children would certainly not participate. That was the last straw.

True to his word their licensor did fly in to meet with the couple and our leadership to bring some closure to the situation and to minister to this couple. Unfortunately, the couple refused to meet with us. The head of their ministry organization attempted to minister to them, but they scorned any correction blaming, of course, the pastors for being unfair and judgmental. They rebuffed their leader and threatened, unwarranted, legal action, so he had no choice but to remove their ministerial license. As is usually the case, this couple had already bonded with certain friends in the church who didn't know all the details, so took their side and left the church. We also had families leave the church who blamed us for having lack of discernment in hiring them in the first place.

There were obviously many demonic strongholds operating in this situation. Steve and I were so naïve. All we wanted to do was provide a wonderful church for people to come and bring their families to receive from God. The enemy made sure however that the spirit of the world, the lust in the world, that carnal, self-centered force would sidetrack our good intentions. It was a powerful wake up call. We had heard news accounts of such instances in secular situations, but we never anticipated facing the potential of that kind of perversion inside our church. We averted the Devolving Culture that time. Little did we know the next scenario would get worse.

And Worse It Got

The third example would prove to be one of the most grave and personally painful experiences of our ministry. We learned that a twenty-two year old young lady who was assisting our youth pastors had developed a sexual relationship with a then fourteen year old boy in the youth group. In parallel, I had watched news coverage of several female teachers having affairs with their young male students. The circumstances and reasoning they describe were eerily similar.

The young lady and her sister had come to our ministry with some worldly baggage, but we had witnessed what we perceived as a genuine transformation in them. Their parents were strong ministry leaders and were thrilled at what God was doing in their daughters' lives. We believed their conversion experience was sincere, but remained disturbed by their provocative dress and behavior. We noticed other young ladies in the church mimicking that "look." It was the same "look" we see on movie and television screens by starlets. My husband would often complain to me that he was tired of looking out from the pulpit, attempting to preach God's Word, and all he could see was cleavage, belly buttons and tight clothing. He insisted that I confront the girls, whom I did, but I was not persuasive. Instead the girls, their parents and others in the youth group seemed to resent my addressing the issue. It was frustrating. We didn't want to appear condemning or prudish, nor did we want to alienate the girls or their family, but they were negatively influencing others. We made a decision to remove the sisters from any type of leadership role. Influence is powerful. Damage we learned later was already done.

When news of this untoward relationship surfaced we understood why we had been sensing such a strong "unclean" spirit in our church. Whichever one of us was preaching at the time would often comment after service, *I don't know why I stressed sexual purity so much. I just couldn't get off the fornication, adultery thing today.* It bothered us. We didn't want to spend so much time harping on the subject, but we couldn't shake it. We did allow the parents of the young lady, because of their ministerial credentials and because it was their daughter involved, to minister to the family of the young man. It was a troubled family with chemical addictions and other family problems. We kept the details as private as possible in order to protect the boy and the families. If we knew then what we know now we would have taken a different course of action. More details came out of the girls taking other teenagers out "clubbing," going from nightclub to bar providing alcohol for the under aged kids. They would show up for services and act very spiritual and allegedly go right back out and do the same thing over and over. One very vulnerable, impressionable young lady, who became part of their entourage, engaged in sexual behavior, ended up pregnant and is today a single mother.

The good news is that we overcame this nightmare of a situation, but not unscathed. The girls and their family turned their pain and anger on us, and once again, we the pastors were said to be the problem in the church. We were too hard, too unfair, too judgmental. They became overtly critical, voicing their criticism of us to others who did not know the seriousness or details of what we were facing. The family gathered a group of members to their "cause" and an insurrection ensued. They and other families left our church, leaving us to pick up the broken and shattered pieces they left behind.

Without Blemish

I pray for all of the people involved in each of the stories I have shared. I pray that they have grown closer to the Lord and have overcome the challenges in their lives. Redemption is a process that is always available and promises that negatives can be turned into positives. I believe the very best for them. My husband and I have definitely received an invaluable education as to the maneuvers of the evil one and are determined not to be blindsided by his tactics again. If we were to survey pastors from all denominations, I believe they would tell similar stories. I don't know of a pastor in our circle that has not had to deal with one or more soap opera scenarios. One pastor's wife coined it, "As the Church Turns." How sad, but again, the church is full of imperfect people and when imperfect people adopt the behaviors of the corrupt culture you have potential of serious problems.

With all its shortcomings the church remains the one ark of safety as well as a school of learning for the Believer. I remember hearing Pastor John Osteen, Joel's father, of Lakewood Church in Houston, Texas, tell that he and his wife Dodie discovered there were people living together, unmarried, in the congregation. Some, he said, had families together. Pastor John, a wonderful man who has since passed on, said that he would line up entire families in the front of the church and marry them all at once. People need the church. They don't need to feel condemned because of their sin, instead they must be instructed and encouraged to live according to the scriptures.

People need the church

God does see us beyond our shortcomings and somehow sees hope for His imperfect church. Amazingly God sees a church without spot or blemish. I don't buy into the thought that we are a post Christian society, because Jesus own words were, *I will build my church; and the gates of hell shall not prevail against it.* (Matthew 16:18 KJV) We are still living out the plan of God and He will have the final say. Darkness will not prevail against the Word of the Living God.

I remain upbeat that the *Un*Cultured Church can be a part of the solution instead of being part of the problem. The *Un*Cultured Church can determine to be the center of God's standards. The *Un*Cultured Church can influence its community with the standards of the scriptures instead of  allowing society to influence it. The *Un*Cultured Church can pray for and support its leaders instead of being critical of them. The *Un*Cultured Church can work with the pastors and leaders to protect the Anointing of the Lord. The *Un*Cultured Church can assist others in recognizing the dangers of the corrupt world around them. The *Un*Cultured Church can obey the great commission of Christ:

> *Then he said, "Go into the world. Go everywhere and announce the Message of God's good news to one and all. Whoever believes and is baptized is saved; whoever refuses to believe is damned. These are some of the signs that will accompany believers: They will throw out demons in my name, they will speak in new tongues, they will take snakes in their hands, they will drink poison and not be hurt, they will lay hands on the sick and make them well." Then the Master Jesus, after briefing them, was taken up to heaven, and he sat down beside God in the place of honor. And the disciples went everywhere preaching, the*

Master working right with them, validating the Message with indisputable evidence.]

Mark 16:15-20 THE MESSAGE BIBLE

We can do it. We can raise the banner of righteousness. We can heed the advice and correction given by God's messengers — His apostles, prophets, evangelists, pastors and teachers. Yes it's dark, but God is Light and in Him is NO darkness.[31] The Light of God has come to dwell within the hearts of men and women. Let's allow the Light of God to shine through us for the world to see. Let's have a revival of sanctification in the church instead of the adoption of oprafication. Let's be the *Un*Cultured Church corporately and individually. In the final chapter, I have some ideas on how we can accomplish that task.

CHAPTER EIGHT

Getting to the Cure

We are living in the most exciting hour of the church. The heroes of our Christian faith, those who have gone on before us, are watching from that great cloud of witnesses the book of Hebrews talks about.[32] They would love to be participating with us in the culmination of events foretold in the scriptures, but all they can do now is cheer us on. This is not the time to be what Patrick Morley calls a cultural Christian.[33]

A cultural Christian is one who is very apathetic about his/her faith. They don't see a necessity to be demonstrative or vocal about their Christian beliefs. They prefer to be a silent believer so that they won't offend others who believe differently. They don't see a necessity for church attendance, and if they do attend it is at their convenience; if they feel like it, if there is a special event, if someone calls and begs them to come. They absolutely will not support the church financially, because all that preacher wants is your money anyway. They figure life is difficult enough without the church making demands on your money and your time. The cultural Christian has without doubt been affected by the Devolving Culture. The Message Bible says,

> Don't become so well-adjusted to your culture that you fit into it without even thinking. Instead, fix your attention on God. You'll be changed from the inside out. Readily recognize what he wants from you, and quickly respond to it. Unlike the culture around you, always dragging you down to its level of immaturity, God brings the best out of you, develops well-formed maturity in you.
>
> Romans 12:2 THE MESSAGE BIBLE

Allowing God to mature you is firstly taking care of the sin problem by accepting Jesus Christ as the Lord and Savior of your life, inviting Him into your heart to forgive you of the SIN you were born into. Secondly, you ask the Holy Spirit to infill and empower you to be the witness you are called to be, so that you can boldly tell others what God has done for you. Thirdly, you get plugged into a life giving church, one that preaches the truth of the Word of God, without compromising, and one where you can exercise your God-given gifts and talents. These three steps are the keys to living the victorious life of faith that the Bible describes. Faith is defined in Hebrews 11:1-2 as,

> Now faith is the substance of things hoped for the evidence of things not seen. For by it the elders obtained a good report.

Faith is always right NOW! It isn't what happened to you years ago, it's always right now. You need faith working for you NOW!

Faith is a real substance, not some ethereal, mystical idea that only a few can understand. It is tangible. You were born with natural faith. You believe a chair will hold you when you sit in it. That's faith. You also were born with spiritual faith to believe in a God you cannot see. Use that faith. Trust in God and allow Him to prove Himself to you.

Faith is the substance of things. God wants to bless you with things…spiritual things, natural things, material things. Faith in God is how you receive them.

Faith is the substance of things hoped for. You've probably had someone tell you, *Don't get your hopes up.* Well, GET YOUR HOPE UP! Hope is earnest expectation. It attaches to faith and brings those things out of the spiritual realm into your natural realm.

Faith is the evidence, the proof positive that God is working on your behalf. The Amplified Bible says that faith is the title deed. It is ownership!

Faith is evidence of things not seen. We cannot always see what God is doing for us, but just as surely as there is a blue sky and green earth, God is working when our faith is activated. Faith is how the elders before us received from God and faith is how we receive from God.

Add to Your Faith

In order to live above the oprahfication of our culture we must live a life of faith in Jesus Christ. Without faith it is impossible to please God. (Hebrews 11:6 KJV) Peter, The Apostle, the same man who denied Christ three times, activated his faith, turned his life around and ended up ministering so effectively

You mean there's more?

to his culture. If an impetuous, hot tempered, man like Peter can do that, there is hope for you and me. He wrote a letter to other Believers and said there are seven things you need to add to your faith. You mean there's more? That's right. I want to end this chapter by challenging us with those seven things.

*And beside this, giving all diligence, add to your faith **virtue;** and to virtue **knowledge;** And to knowledge **temperance;** and to temperance **patience;** and to patience **godliness;** And to godliness **brotherly kindness;** and to brotherly kindness **charity.** For if these things be in you, and abound, they make you that ye shall neither be barren nor unfruitful in the knowledge of our Lord Jesus Christ.*

2 Peter 1:5-8 KJV

Virtue

The Greek word "virtue"[34] used by Peter in this scripture means excellence and praise and is further defined as moral and sexual purity.[35] My husband has taught for years that excellence does not mean being perfect always. Excellence is a spirit, a way of thinking, of doing the best with the materials and resources at hand. He also says that "praise" is the word "raise" with a "p" on the front of it. Praise should raise you up; therefore, a virtuous person should have an attitude of going to the highest level of excellence. While the Devolving Culture depicts grey areas of sexual conduct, Peter was saying that we should have the highest degree of morality. God's Word is explicit.

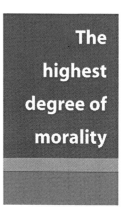

> *The Spirit makes it clear that as time goes on, some are going to **give up on the faith and chase after demonic illusions put forth by professional liars.** These liars have lied so well and for so long that they've lost their capacity for truth. **They will tell you not to get married.***
>
> Timothy 4:1-3 THE MESSAGE

We have already established the fact that the Devolving Culture no longer places importance on marriage or abstaining from sex until you are married. The new cultural code defines sexual morality as having sex with someone you love; boyfriend/girlfriend, man/man, woman/woman. This is in direct contradiction to scriptural teachings. According to Webster's Dictionary, fornication means human sexual intercourse other than between a man and a WIFE.[36] God has established the covenant of marriage as the only parameter for sexual behavior and the Bible is specific about avoiding fornication.

> **1 Corinthians 6:13 KJV** *...Now the body is not for **fornication,** but for the Lord; and the Lord for the body.*
>
> **1 Corinthians 6:18 KJV** *Flee fornication. Every sin that a man doeth is without the body; but **he that committeth fornication sinneth against his own body.***
>
> **1 Corinthians 6:18 THE MESSAGE BIBLE** *There is a sense in which sexual sins are different from all others. **In sexual sin we violate the sacredness of our own bodies,** these bodies that were made for God-given and God-modeled love, for "becoming one" with another.*

1 Corinthians 7:1, 2 THE MESSAGE BIBLE *Now, getting down to the questions you asked in your letter to me. First, Is it a good thing to have sexual relations? Certainly—but only within a certain context.* **It's good for a man to have a wife, and for a woman to have a husband.** *Sexual drives are strong, but marriage is strong enough to contain them and provide for a balanced and fulfilling sexual life in a world of sexual disorder.*

Galatians 5:19-21 KJV *Now the works of the flesh are manifest, which are these; Adultery,* **fornication,** *uncleanness, lasciviousness, Idolatry, witchcraft, hatred, variance, emulations, wrath, strife, seditions, heresies, Envyings, murders, drunkenness, revellings, and such like: of the which I tell you before, as I have also told you in time past, that they which do such things shall not inherit the kingdom of God.*

* Note-fornication is listed with every other sinful vice which will cause disinheritance with God.

Ephesians 5:3 KJV *But* **fornication,** *and all uncleanness, or covetousness,* **let it not be once named among you,** *as becometh saints;*

1 Thessalonians 4:3 KJV *For this is the will of God, even your sanctification, that ye should* **abstain from fornication:**

Fornication is sexual impurity of all kinds. The current morality code also expects Christians to embrace or at least be tolerant of those who have an affinity toward persons of the same sex. Christians are taught to do what Jesus does—love the sinner and hate the sin. There is no confusion at all in the scriptures concerning homosexual behavior. Some cultural elite in the medical and educational fields will argue that these people are born with a predisposed attraction, that they can't help themselves. Whether this is a learned behavior or the cause of a spiritual influence, the only thing we know for certain is that men are born with an X and a Y chromosome and women are born with two X chromosomes. It doesn't matter what kind of sex change or what part of anatomy is surgically altered, whatever sex you were born with you will die with, because it's in your DNA. You cannot change the sex you were born with, but you can change the exterior and you can change the behavior. God's Word has specific instructions for sexual behavior and the Bible calls homosexual acts SIN.

> **Leviticus 18:22 Message Bible** *Don't have sex with a man as one does with a woman.* ***That is abhorrent.***

> **Leviticus 20:13 Message Bible** *If a man has sex with a man as one does with a woman, both of them have done* ***what is abhorrent.***

> **Romans 1:25-28** AMP *Because they exchanged the truth of God for a lie and worshiped and served the creature rather than the Creator…God gave them over and abandoned them to **vile affections** and **degrading passions**. For their women exchanged their natural function for an unnatural and abnormal one, And the men also turned from natural relations with women and were set ablaze (burning out, consumed) with lust for one another—men committing shameful acts with men and **suffering in their own bodies and personalities** the inevitable consequences and penalty of their wrong-doing… And so, since they did not see fit to acknowledge God or approve of Him or consider Him worth the knowing, God gave them over to a base and condemned mind **to do things not proper or decent but loathsome,***

Isn't it interesting that virtue, sexual purity, is the first thing that Peter said we must add to our faith in Jesus Christ.

I hear the excuses of the Devolving Culture; people can't help themselves, people need sex, people are going to be sexually active, you can't stop sexual activity. There is a very simple solution to each of these. It is one of the nine fruits of the Holy Spirit—SELF CONTROL. Yes, it is actually one of the benefits of being filled with God's Holy Spirit. You can control your own passions and wrong desires. You can take authority over thoughts implanted that when acted upon become sin in your life. You can ask God to forgive you and to help you make the right choices. 1 John 1:9 KJV says, *If we confess our sins, he is faithful and just to forgive us our sins, and to cleanse us from all unrighteousness.*

Covenant is God's plan

I know that in today's cultural climate it may not be fashionable to admit that you are a sinner, but you need to examine your own life. There are decisions you can make to insure that you are on the right side of God's Word. Are you single and involved sexually with someone? Break if off. Stop it. That's right. You are in control of that decision. Are you living with someone you are not married to? Do you love that person? Is that person your life's partner or are you just involved because of the sex? If you love that person and you know that they are your partner for life, then do the right thing. Enter into the covenant relationship of marriage. Covenant is God's plan. That's what He did for you when He gave His life. He fulfilled His covenant of blessing and He wants to bless your relationships. If that person is not your life's partner then move out. Are you involved in a homosexual or lesbian affair? Please allow the Word of God to speak to you. God loves you. He will help you overcome wrong, lustful desires and give you a fulfilling and completed life.

Add to your faith—virtue.

Knowledge

Opinions are a dime a dozen. Everybody has one. People are usually more than willing to express their point of view, but I have found that it is important to be equipped with facts when I need to make important decisions in my life. The Greek word for knowledge in this scripture means to know the science or the facts.[37] Knowing the facts of what God's Word says about something rather than what someone's opinion is or what the culture dictates is vital. The Book of Corinthians gives us a sound method;

> [Inasmuch as we] refute arguments and theories and reasonings and every proud and lofty thing that sets itself up against the [true] knowledge of God; and we **lead every thought and purpose away captive** into the obedience of Christ (the Messiah, the Anointed One),
>
> 2 Corinthians 10:5 AMP

Thoughts come and go from the world around you, your friends and family, and even from the devil himself. Paul called these thoughts "vain imaginations."[38] We are instructed to take these thoughts captive. How do we do that? As soon as a thought comes into your life replace it with what God says. Here's where knowing the scriptures is so important. When you hear the Word and believe the Word it is the Word that is going to come out of your mouth. The Word you speak will overcome any wrong thought. If you haven't memorized scriptures then get the Bible out and just read it out loud, but purpose to become a student of the Word of God. Have your own Bible study or join a Bible study group or make sure that you are part of a church that gives good Bible teaching. Get the facts.

Add to virtue — knowledge.

Temperance

I am an avid chocoholic. I love rich dark chocolate made with fine organic ingredients. Chocolate has to be tempered, that is heated and stirred to the right consistency. Sometimes I feel like my life is like chocolate being tempered, when problems act like fire to heat and melt and pressure stirs the pot of my spirit. I know the heat is there so that I can be tempered. I need it even though I would prefer to avoid stressful situations of conflict. To temper something also means to render moderation.[39] Peter used the Greek word for temperance[40] which means moderation or self control — one of the fruits of the Spirit, which we have already discussed. In all our lives we will face circumstances that are strenuous, but we can turn these into positive life lessons by receiving and demonstrating the fruits of the Spirit which are love, joy, peace, longsuffering, gentleness, goodness, faith, meekness and finally temperance. (Galatians 5:22, 23 KJV)

*For God did not give us a spirit of timidity (of cowardice, of craven and cringing and fawning fear), but [He has given us a spirit] of power and of love and of calm and well-balanced mind and discipline and **self-control.***

2 Timothy 1:7 AMP

Fear is the enemy of our faith. It is essentially the opposite of faith or faith in the opposite direction. Fear will always go 180 degrees in the other direction against God and His Word. Fear of failure, fear of disappointment, fear of rejection—fear is not our friend. Fear is what causes us to distrust and act in unbelief. God has not given us that spirit of fear. The spirit of fear always comes from the enemy. God has given us His power and love to overcome our own fear oriented thoughts and the fear based actions of others. So no matter what circumstance you are facing, no matter what difficult decision you may have to make, take authority over the fear and trust in God. Receive His gift of a calm and well-balanced mind. You have a brain. Use it. Your soul (mind, will and emotions) is a gift from the Almighty. You have an intellect to reason and process information. Make sure you have the correct information. You have a will to decide. God gave you the ability to choose for yourself and you can control your emotions in the process. Your emotions don't have to control you. God has given you the ability to discipline your thoughts and behavior by using His power of self control. Control yourself with the Word of God.

Add to knowledge—temperance.

Patience

The Online Etymology Dictionary describes patience as the "quality of being patient in suffering; to quietly and steadily persevere."[41] There is an old joke that says *Lord, give me patience and give it to me NOW!* Peter used the Greek word for patience[42] which has a more in depth meaning; to be cheerful, to be hopeful, and to have endurance and constancy. God expects us to keep our attitude in tune with His Holy Spirit who sees the end from the beginning (Isaiah 46:10 KJV). He already knows how the situation will turn out and He's not worried. Even when we have made wrong choices and messed up our lives, the Father God still has our best interest at heart. He is working all things together for our good (Romans 8:28). Patience is a powerful weapon to use against the enemy of God. Satan does his best to destroy our confidence by piling on pressure, but when we smile and laugh and dance, it sends confusion to his camp. So show some teeth, stay steady and shame the devil.

> *...let patience have her perfect work, that ye may be perfect and entire, wanting nothing.*
>
> James 1:4 KJV

Add to temperance—patience.

Godliness

Godliness by both modern definition and by the original Greek word simply means holiness.[43] Holiness is doing things God's way, when He says and how He says to do it. It is God's way of doing and being right (Romans 6:19 AMP). I was reared in a Pentecostal church and in the early years of its existence the denomination had strict regulations on, not only conduct, but clothing and attire. The church did not allow women to cut their hair, wear trousers or make-up, and I have to admit to you those were some of the homeliest women you've ever seen. I could not comprehend how the men could dress

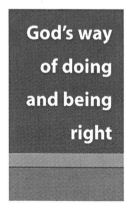

really sharp, but their wives had to be dowdy. The church elders considered these rules as standards of holiness. We now understand that their ideal of holiness came from a religious spirit and a lack of understanding of true holiness. My grand-father, our pastor, who never towed the legalistic line, used to tell us, *Put some lipstick on girls. Even an old barn needs a fresh coat of paint every now and then.*

Holiness or godliness is an attitude and a decision to obey God's Word, although it does encompass modesty in dress and behavior. A woman of God should not look like a street walker or dress provocatively. It is possible to wear current fashion and not have people think, *What is she selling?* A catch phrase repeated in this Devolving Culture is "sexy." Advertisers target consumers with "sexy" products to help people look and be "sexy." Women and men of God, however, should desire to demonstrate who they are inside and outside. We are the beau-tiful embodiment of God's glory. We turn heads when we walk into a room, because we shine with divine charisma. We operate our lives with integrity and the character of God. We comport our daily affairs with honesty and truthfulness. Business associates and friends know they can depend on us to keep our word. We heed the Bible's words about avoiding coarse talk and vulgarity (Ephesians 5:4 KJV). Before attending secular events or venues, we ask ourselves, *What would Jesus do?*

> *For God hath not called us unto uncleanness, but unto **holiness.***
>
> Thessalonians 4:7 KJV

> *Having therefore these promises, dearly beloved, let us cleanse ourselves from all filthiness of the flesh and spirit, **perfecting holiness** in the fear of God.*
>
> 2 Corinthians 7:1

Add to patience — godliness.

Brotherly Kindness

Jesus taught His disciples to do for others what you want them to do for you. He said this one principle sums up all that is written in the Law and the books of the Prophets (Matthew 7:12 THE MESSAGE Bible). Oh, that men would heed the words of Christ. A kind word, a kind gesture, an act of kindness should be a way of life for believing Believers. Peter encouraged us[44] to be generous to our fellow Christians and Paul said we should be especially so to those, "...who are of the household of faith. " (Galatians 6:10)

All too often though churches are filled with gossiping, slandering, backbiting, tale-bearing, critical and sharp tongued members. The Devolving Culture is so inundated with salacious media coverage of public figures, generating a pungent stench of filthy conversation that has seeped into church life. It's outrageous. Some Christians don't think twice before repeating filthy accusations about church members, pastors and leaders. My mother taught me, *If you can't say anything nice, don't say anything at all.* The difference in churches is that we cloak our gossip with the guise of concern and the need to pray for that person. My husband admonishes new members when they join our church that it is not generally immorality or financial problems that destroys churches. It is *loose lips that sink ships.* In front of our entire congregation he encourages new members that if anyone at any time speaks ill or critically of someone in our church, they have his permission to stop them mid-sentence and say, *Let's pray for them right now.* Then go with that individual to the person they are speaking of and address the problem with them face to face.

How many churches have been destroyed because of strife? How many people have been disaffected and dropped out of church because of their disappointment and disgust with some Christian's behavior? The book of Proverbs lists seven things that God hates (Proverbs 6:15-19 KJV) and the seventh one He calls an abomination—a vile abhorrent sinful act. The seventh is sowing discord among the brethren. Did you get that? God likens sowing discord to his hatred of fornication, homosexuality and other sexual sins. Some of the same prideful Christians who will picket abortion clinics and protest gay pride parades will enter into the House of the Lord and commit a sin that is just as vile in the eyes of God. We need to walk the love walk, not only with unbelievers and non Christians but with our brothers and sisters in Christ. *Let brotherly love continue* (Hebrews 13:1 KJV). The Amplified Bible says, *LET LOVE for your fellow believers continue and be a fixed practice with you [never let it fail].* Ask yourself, How would I want to be treated? How would Jesus treat them? Then conduct your conversation and decisions based on the love walk He demonstrated.

> *We know that we have passed over out of death into Life by the fact that we **love the brethren** (our fellow Christians). He who does not love abides (remains, is held and kept continually) in [spiritual] death.*
>
> 1 John 3:14 AMP

Add to godliness — brotherly kindness.

Charity

> I believe in Love. I believe He's God.
> I believe that Love never fails.
> I believe that Truth will prevail.
> Love conquers all my fear.
> Truth is the Word I hear.
> Faith speaks it loud and clear.
> That's why I believe.[45]

The Greek word Peter used for charity[46] is the word love which specifically means benevolence or helping others who cannot help themselves. It literally means to have a love feast in giving to those in need, to go over the top in extending aid, comfort and security. God is Love (1 John 4:8 KJV). He loved us when we were in need of a Savior, when we were lost and going to a devil's hell. In the heart of every born again believer is Love that wants to reach out and pull someone else out of the gutter of despair, to assist them in turning their lives around Yes, we should provide food, shelter and financial assistance. Jesus said, *And whoever gives to one of these little ones [in rank or influence] even a cup of cold water because he is My disciple, surely I declare to you, he shall not lose his reward.* Matthew 10:42 AMP

While we provide for natural aid, we also give people the bread of life, a way out of the void of spiritual despair. We preach the Good News that Jesus came to seek and to save that which was lost (Luke 19:10). The old song *Amazing Grace* says, "I once was lost but now I'm found, was blind but now I see."[47] Are we doing enough to reach out to our fellow man? Are we giving to charities and tithing and helping our churches? Are we serving as volunteers in our communities? Are we being the witness that Christ commanded? Are we demonstrating the Love of God to others around us? St. Francis of Assisi is quoted as saying, *Preach the Gospel at all times and when necessary use words.*[48]

Love is a powerful force, the only real weapon Christians have in fighting the cultural war, because the tools of our warfare are spiritual not natural. This war of words and ideologies between the Devolving Culture and our Christian values can only be won by appropriating Christ's example. The following Love

Love is a powerful force

Confession, taken from 1 Corinthians 13:4-8 AMP, is a tremendous tool in our arsenal that my husband and I learned early on in ministry. It has proven invaluable over the years in keeping our spirituality, integrity, and sanity intact. I highly recommend that you read it, confess it out loud and commit it to memory. I am leaving a blank for you to insert your name in place of the word "love."

Love Confession

Love_____(your name)_____ endures long and is patient and kind;

_____ never is envious nor boils over with jealousy,

_____ is not boastful or vainglorious,

_____ does not display itself (herself/himself) haughtily.

_____ is not conceited (arrogant and inflated with pride);

_____ is not rude (unmannerly) and does not act unbecomingly.

_____ does not insist on its (her/his) own rights or its (her/his) own way,

_____ is not self-seeking;

_____ is not touchy or fretful or resentful;

_____ takes no account of the evil done to it (her/him)

_____ pays no attention to a suffered wrong.

_____ does not rejoice at injustice and unrighteousness, but _____ rejoices when right and truth prevail.

_____ bears up under anything and everything that comes,

_____ is ever ready to believe the best of every person,

_____'s hopes are fadeless under all circumstances, and

_____ endures everything [without weakening].

_____ never fails.

Add to brotherly kindness — love.

CHAPTER NINE

Sanctification

I am reminded of another *Saturday Night Live* skit called "The Church Lady." The character was a man dressed in drag who religiously berated all his guests, pompously pointing out their obvious sins, and the punch line was, *Isn't that special?* I would not at all be surprised to have many in the Devolving Culture label me as that church lady or at least place me in the category of a prudish zealot. Regardless, I will be walking the love walk. I will walk in love with those who ridicule, persecute and dismiss the values we believing Believers hold dearly.

Probably like you, I have loved ones who are not totally enlightened to the truth of the Gospel message, and it hurts my heart to see them succumb to the deceptions of evaporating standards in moral conduct. I will continue to believe the very best for each, to pray for their spiritual eyes to be opened (Ephesians 1:18). I will never cease my high expectation that each will realize the void in their hearts and allow Christ to fill it. I refuse to be the voice of condemnation, but rather I am determined to comport myself as Jesus did, loving them in the

The Oprah mantra

midst of their poor decisions, being a support when they reap the harvest of bad seeds sown, and provide answers for REAL change.

I will not be a silent cultural Christian. I will not stand by while the world around us dissolves into a decadent moral chasm, and I will not fall in line with the Oprah mantra simply because she is a wonderful likeable person. I will shout out loud to anyone who will listen, *Wake up! Does Oprah Winfrey have more credibility than God?* Oprahfication endorses cohabitation in place of the covenant of marriage, homosexual partnerships and the accompanying lifestyle, and ideologies engrained in the metaphysical New Age movement. Oprahfication means not necessarily embracing these beliefs but having apathy toward them along with a slow acceptance. To solidify my point, just today I took a break and with remote in hand turned on Oprah's show. She was interviewing a forty-ish woman stripper, a mother of a thirteen year old girl. The woman looked like the typical suburban housewife next door. The fact that this woman is a stripper and not a "showroom model" as she has declared is being revealed before millions of people on television. Oprah asks her how she feels about people discovering her real occupation, about how she thinks her daughter will now be received by other children and families in the community. Is she concerned that her daughter will be mocked and ostracized? The woman expresses some concern but is proud of how she provides for her family and describes what she does as giving comfort to family type men who just need to relieve stress before they go home to their wives. Give me a major break. The thirteen year old via video states that she is proud of her mother and their unique family. Then Oprah says something to the effect, *You know people are going to judge, because they judge.* The correspondent who had brought the story chimed in something like, *And we really shouldn't judge.*

While it is true that Jesus told us not to judge lest we be judged,[49] it is also true that he never swept sin under the rug and He never condoned sin. He told the prostitute that her sins were forgiven and, *Go and sin no more!* I was screaming at the TV set, *The woman takes her clothes off in front of men. Is that a good example for a thirteen year old impressionable young girl? Why don't you talk about the consequences of being in that seedy environment? Talk about the activities that go along with strip clubs—drug use, prostitution and other illegal operations! Talk about lives that have been destroyed, families torn apart!* How poignant. Oprah's program once again underscored for me that the Devolving Culture's terminologies have different definitions from our Christian values. When the culture says, *Don't judge,* they mean, *Accept it, because all opinions and all behaviors are equal.* Christians can love and respect people without accepting their behavior or endorsing it by default. By that I mean when we say nothing, when we shrug our shoulders, walk away and go to our "bless me" church services we are leaving the culture to decide that our views are not relevant. We must be proactive.

More New Age Doctrine

It also is NO SECRET that Oprah Winfrey is entangled, and has been for quite some time, with New Age philosophies. Years ago I viewed a program in which she invited certain New Age leadership to explain the method of "channeling" spirit guides, and she even had several "mediums" demonstrate their powers to allow these "spirits" to speak through them. As a Christian, I watched with dismay recognizing that true "mediums" conjure up demon "spirits." I remember thinking, *This is nothing to be playing around with!* Oprah seemed, at first, to be enamored with and approving until she pressed one of them to "channel" their "spirit" on national television. The "medium" went into a supposed deep trance revealing that another "being" had taken over her body and a gruff, hoarse, manly voice erupted from this demure female frame. It was obviously contrived and Oprah appeared embarrassed. I thought, *Surely she can see through this New Age nonsense,* however she has continued to explore false anti-Christ doctrines.

Marianne Williamson is an Oprah friend who has been speaking into Oprah's life for a number of years. Ms. Williamson, a premier New Age leader and currently a reporter on "Oprah and Friends," Oprah's XM Satellite Radio Network, is also a noted guest on her television program. She is presented as being wise, intellectual and profound. In my opinion, her teaching is not so innocent, but, in fact, is subtle, deceiving and diabolically inspired. At the time of this writing, she has been selected to take the listeners on a daily journey of

A Course in Miracles,[50] a 365 day lesson curriculum with workbook included, that encourages people to rethink everything they believe about God and life. "The *Course* Workbook bluntly states: "**This is a course in mind training**"[51] and is dedicated to "**thought reversal.**"[52] *A Course in Miracles*,[53] fast becoming the bible of the New Age movement, is a compilation of teachings by Helen Schucman, a Columbia University Professor of Medical Psychology, who purportedly received new revelations from "Jesus" to help humanity through these difficult times. "Jesus" spoke to her and told her to write down, dictate, the new thinking he was revealing. Her revelations of "Jesus" bear no resemblance to Christ our Savior. Warren Smith, a former New Age follower, outlines some of these dangerous teachings:

- "There is **no sin**. . . "
- A "slain Christ has **no meaning.**"
- "The journey to the cross should be the last **useless** journey."
- "Do not make the pathetic error of 'clinging to the old rugged cross.'"
- "The Name of Jesus Christ as such is but a symbol... It is a symbol that is safely used as a replacement for the many names of **all the gods to which you pray.**"
- "**God is in everything** I see."
- "The recognition of **God is** the recognition of **yourself.**"

- "The oneness of the Creator and the creation is your wholeness, your sanity and your limitless power."

- "The Atonement is the final lesson he [man] need learn, for it teaches him that, never having sinned, he has no need of salvation."[54]

These teachings are blasphemous

Undoubtedly, these teachings are blasphemous. When you remove sin from the equation you discharge the need for a Savior and the sacrifice He made—the blood that He shed and the stripes He bore on His body. When you denigrate the Name of God you erase the importance of Him being the One, True, and Holy God. Jesus Christ, God Incarnate, warned that this would occur in the last days.

*If anyone says to you then, Behold, here is the Christ (the Messiah)! or, There He is!—do not believe it. For **false Christs** and **false prophets will arise**, and they will show great signs and wonders **so as to deceive and lead astray**, if possible, even the elect (God's chosen ones). See, I have warned you beforehand.*

Matthew 24:23-25 AMP

Posted on Oprah's official website, is the daily lesson by Marianne Williamson along with a passage from the workbook. The following quote ought to ring alarm bells in the thoughts and hearts of every born again child of God:

"Some of the ideas the workbook presents **you will find hard to believe,** and others may seem to be **quite startling.**

This does not matter. You are merely asked to **apply the ideas** as you are directed to do. **You are not asked to judge them at all.** You are asked only to **use them.** It is their use that will give them meaning to you, and will show you that they are true.

Remember only this; **you need not believe the ideas, you need not accept them, and you need not even welcome them. Some of them you may actively resist. None of this will matter,** or decrease their efficacy. But do not allow yourself to make exceptions in applying the ideas the workbook contains, and **whatever your reactions to the ideas may be, use them.** Nothing more than that is required (Workbook, p. 2)."

—Excerpted from *A Course in Miracles*

New Age ideologues, false prophets, expect us to comply with outright anti-Christian doctrine that is unbelievable and is quite blasphemously shocking, because, after all, THEY are the supposed enlightened ones. Again, the Devolving Culture wants to erode judgment. Don't judge, just do it. Why? This is how the devil operates. He comes to steal, kill and to destroy. A wrong thought implanted in your thinking (your soul—mind, will and emotions) will take root and incubate bringing doubt and unbelief. Soon you will begin to question even the soundest of Biblical teachings. That is the enemy's objective. He will steal the WORD of God from your mind, then come in for the kill and ultimately destroy your faith in God.

In Chapter Five, we discussed the ancient roots of these devilish ideas; that there are many Gods; that certain people have esoteric knowledge or revelations; that the main God at the center is YOU; that man is a god unto himself. The demons that inspired the doctrines of the Gnostics and the Antimonians are alive and actively inspiring those in modern Monism and Pantheism and this satanically based mindset is apparently being propagated by television's media mogul, Oprah Winfrey. Christians are among the starry-eyed, or should I say, blind-eyed, followers.

What Should We Do?

Oprah Winfrey is a well meaning good person, but being a good person is not enough, according to the scriptures and Jesus' own words, *Marvel not that I said unto thee, Ye must be born again.* (John 3:7 KJV) Before you can be born again, you must recognize that you need a Savior. You cannot save yourself. You are not innately good. You were born with a sin nature. When a person is born of the Spirit of God there is a spiritual cleansing that takes place. It's akin to being filthy dirty and standing under a long hot shower. God just washes all that stink and grime and leaves you with the clean fragrance of His abiding forgiving love. A born again child of God strives to please Him and cherishes His Word above any and all worldly opinions. Likewise, when a Christian is sanctified we stand under the shower and allow Him to purge us of wrong influences, motives and behaviors. Throughout our Christian experience we will come back to the sanctification shower because,

> *Christ also loved the church, and gave himself for it;*
> *That he might **sanctify and cleanse it with the washing of***
> ***water by the word,** That he might present it to himself a glorious*

church, not having spot, or wrinkle, or any such thing; but that it should be holy and without blemish.

Ephesians 5:26, 27 KJV

If we will hold fast to God's Word, which is alive and active (Hebrews 4:12 AMP), it will cleanse us from all unrighteousness (1 John 1:19). We cannot cleanse ourselves. No self help guru or personal life coach can bring deep, pure and permanent cleansing. Only Jesus Christ, the Son of God, has the power to revolutionize a person from the inside outward. Only  Christ can expose the roots and remove the sin, which is the cause of all immorality. A personal, intimate and life long relationship with Jesus Christ is the cure.

I am not a theologian, but I am a student of the Word of God, and I am a pastor. As such, I have an obligation to express the truth and to expose the enemy's tactics. I pray for Oprah Winfrey that the scales of deception will be removed from her spiritual eyes, that she will return to the true God of the Bible — Jesus Christ — and make Him the Lord of her life. I remain optimistic that God will continue to do marvelous signs and miracles through believing Believers and establish a glorious Church in the midst of a perverse society. The Church of Jesus Christ is the most dynamic entity on the planet. Christians are to BE Christ to a lost and dying world. We have more influence than we give ourselves credit. With the influx of Christian programming media we have a spirited and boisterous voice.

We are a tremendous voting block. We can make a difference. We can live in this troubled, sin riddled, confused, hell bound world without being a part of it. Jesus prayed a prayer to His Father God,

> *I have given and delivered to them Your word (message) and the world has hated them, because **they are not of the world** [do not belong to the world], just as I am not of the world. I do not ask that You will take them out of the world, but that You will keep and protect them from the evil one. **They are not of the world** (worldly, belonging to the world), [just] as I am not of the world. **Sanctify them** [purify, consecrate, separate them for Yourself, make them holy] by the Truth; **Your Word is Truth.** Just as You sent Me into the world, I also have sent them into the world.*
>
> John 17:14-18 AMP

We are IN the world but not OF the world, and we should daily strive for sanctification instead of oprahfication. I leave you with one of my favorite scriptures,

> *Create in me a clean heart, O God; and renew a right spirit within me.*
>
> Psalm 51:10 KJV

PRAYER OF SALVATION

Romans 10 verses 8, 9 and 10 state that if you believe in your heart and confess with your mouth that God has raised Christ from the dead you will be saved. Being born again is inviting Jesus Christ to come into your spirit-man and live inside you. You can invite Him into your heart by saying the following prayer:

> *Lord, I believe that you sent your Son, Jesus Christ, to die on the cross for my sins. I believe that you raised Christ from the dead and He lives now. Jesus, I believe you died for my sins. Please forgive me of the sin in my life. I repent of every wrong thought and deed. I denounce sin and its consequences. Come into my life and change me from the inside out. I invite you now to be the Savior and Lord of my life. From this moment forward I declare that I am saved. I am a Christian. I am born again. Holy Spirit, fill me with Your power that I may be the witness You have called me to be. Thank-you Lord for your saving grace!*

Welcome to the family of God. Get a good Bible and start reading. I suggest you begin with the New Testament. Allow the Word of God to transform your thoughts and way of living. Find a good Bible believing, Spirit-filled, church and get active in the Kingdom of God. Today begins your best life ever!

ENDNOTES

1   Scripture Reference— Romans 10:14

2   Scripture Reference— John 8: 3-11

3   Scripture Reference—John, Chapter 4

4   1969 Thomas Harris, Harper and Row

5   2006 Josh D. McDowell and David H. Bellis, Green Key Books

6   ibid

7   ibid

8   Scripture Reference—Matthew, Chapter 24

9   Scripture Reference—Luke 11:33

10 February 15-17, 2008, Rochelle Sharpe, America by the Numbers, Out of Wedlock Births, Single and now a mom, USA Weekend

11 Scripture Reference— Genesis Chapters 1-3

12 Scripture Reference— Isaiah 14:12

13 Scripture Reference— Revelation 12:4, Isaiah 14:12-14, 2 Peter 2:4, Jude 6, Romans 8:20

14 Scripture Reference— Luke 10:18

15 Scripture Reference— Hebrews 3:1, 2

16 Scripture Reference— Psalm 68: 18, Ephesians 4:8, Matthew 16:19, Revelation 1:18

17 Scripture Reference— Mark 16:15

18 2008 Phil Cooke, Branding Faith, Why Some Churches and Non Profits Impact Culture and Others Don't, Regal/Gospel Light

[19] Scripture Reference— 2 Thessalonians 2:3

[20] Scripture Reference— 1 Timothy 4:1

[21] March 5, 2007, Peter Birkenhead, Oprah's ugly secret, salon.com

[22] 1910, Wallace Wattles, The Science of Getting Rich, Public Domain

[23] 2008, thesecret.tv, home page

[24] 2007, Rod Parsley, Culturally Incorrect, Thomas Nelson, page 60

[25] James Strong, The Exhaustive Concordance of The Bible, Greek #4982

[26] 2006, WordNet 3.0, Princeton University

[27] Scripture Reference— Ephesians 5:27

[28] January, 2008, Michelle Van Loon, Willow Creek Pastor Admits 'Mistake', Charisma Magazine

[29] ibid

[30] Scripture Reference— 1 Thessalonians 5:22

[31] Scripture Reference— 1 John 1:5

[32] Scripture Reference— Hebrews 12:1

[33] 1989, Patrick Morley, the Man in the Mirror, Zondervan Publishing

[34] James Strong, The Exhaustive Concordance of The Bible, Greek #703

[35] 1916, Webster's Seventh New Collegiate Dictionary, G. & C. Merriam Co.

[36] ibid

[37] James Strong, The Exhaustive Concordance of The Bible, Greek #1108

[38] Scripture Reference— Romans 1:21

[39] 2008, Dictionary.com Unabridged (v 1.1)

[40] James Strong, The Exhaustive Concordance of The Bible, Greek #1466

[41] 2008, Online Etymology Dictionary

[42] James Strong, The Exhaustive Concordance of The Bible, Greek #5281

[43] James Strong, The Exhaustive Concordance of The Bible, Greek #2150

[44] James Strong, The Exhaustive Concordance of The Bible, Greek #5360

[45] 2008, Cheryl Ingram, I Believe In Love, Psalmist Covenant Publishing

[46] James Strong, The Exhaustive Concordance of The Bible, Greek #26

[47] Public Domain

[48] 2008, brainyquote.com

[49] Scripture Reference— Matthew 7:1

[50] 1975, *A Course in Miracles: Combined Volume* (Glen Ellen, California: Foundation for Inner Peace)

[51] November 2007, Warren Smith, "Oprah and Friends" to teach course on New Age Christ, crossroadto/articles

[52] ibid

[53] ibid

[54] ibid

ABOUT THE AUTHOR

Cheryl Ingram became a dedicated follower of Christ after her first year at Michigan State University. As a theater major, she briefly attended Wayne State University in Detroit, Michigan before transferring to Lee University in Cleveland, Tennessee. It was at the small Christian college that Cheryl initially met her husband, Steve, who was the guest speaker at a chapel service. From there she was enlisted as a summer volunteer at the outreach ministry of Surfside Challenge in Miami, Florida, where Steve had developed the Parable Coffeehouse in Coconut Grove.

Steve and Cheryl married in 1973 and, along with others, formed the music group "Alpenglow," one of the pioneering contemporary Christian bands. They were regulars on the Christian Broadcasting Network's "700 Club" television program and recorded on the "Housetop" record label. When her husband accepted the position as music director for singer/speaker Kenneth Copeland, she became a back-up singer and soloist for his ministry as well as performing for other churches, conventions, concerts and television shows worldwide. Cheryl is a singer/songwriter and has recorded many music products.

After traveling in their own music and teaching ministry, the Ingrams birthed Word of Faith Family Church in Daytona Beach, Florida and the IMI School of Ministry and Music. Steve and Cheryl Ingram are the Senior Pastor and Co-Pastor and are founding instructors in the school of ministry. Together, they host a weekly television program entitled, *You'll Never Be the Same Again.* In addition to being a teacher/preacher, she hosts the Daytona WOW Women of the Word and YWOW Young Women of the Word organization. WOW's focus has been to give all women, single or married, an encouraging avenue to grow in the Lord through Godly relationships and interaction with other strong role models. She has also authored the book, *When God Calls He Anoints.* You may contact Cheryl Ingram at:

Ingram Ministries

P. O. Box 10261

Daytona Beach, Florida 32120

386-255-0662

www.woffcdaytonabeach.org